Marijuana

Indoor Cultivation

A Reference
Manual with
Step-by-Step
Instructions

Marijuana New School

Indoor Cultivation

Jeff Mowta

A Reference
Manual with
Step-by-Step
Instructions

Green Candy Press

Published by Green Candy Press
San Francisco, CA
www.greencandypress.com
ISBN 10: 1-931160-42-2
ISBN 13: 978-1-931160-42-1

Marijuana New School Indoor Cultivation: A Reference Manual with Step-by-Step Instructions, by Jeff Mowta.

Printed in Canada
Sometimes massively distributed by P.G.W.

This book contains information about illegal substances specifically the plant Cannabis Sativa and its derivative products. Green Candy Press would like to emphasize that cannabis is a controlled substance in North America and throughout much of the world. As such, the use and cultivation of cannabis can carry heavy penalties that may threaten an individual's liberty and livelihood.

The aim of the Publisher is to educate and entertain. Whatever the Publisher's view on the validity of current legislation, we do not in any way condone the use of prohibited substances.

Contents

Chapter 5
Maintaining the
Grow Room 181

Chapter 6
Harvesting, Drying, and
Storing 227

Chapter 7
Breeding 234

Chapter 8
Composting 243

Chapter 9
Troubleshooting 249

Glossary 255

Index 260

1

Growing with Seeds

The Starter Room

This section is about closet growing with regard to using minimal space to start seedlings, make clones, or to grow a little bit of bud. Fluorescent lights or halide lights can be used for raising seedlings, growing mother plants for clones, or for budding plants.

Fluorescent Closet System

The chief advantage of fluorescent lights, especially Envirolites, is that they don't generate too much heat, which means that a grower can get away with using the following materials.

Materials

A. Fluorescent lights (tubes or Envirolites). Requirements: If tubes are used, they should fit in the desired space. If Envirolites are used, one 95-watt bulb is used for every 2.6 square feet of growing space for vegetative growth and mother plants.

B. A custom gardening system for the desired space (chapter 4 has a complete list of parts and instructions for building a system for any room size). Flood and drain is best for seedlings.

C. Smell removal system (if necessary). Items of removal in the grow room are ionizers and air neutralizing agents such as Ona.

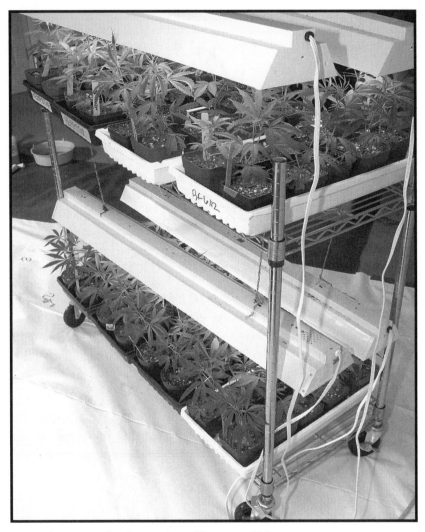

Young plants started under two tiers of fluorescent lights.

Maintenance

All maintenance instructions for vegetative and flowering growth are given in chapter 5.

Metal Halide Closet System

Materials

1. 400 to 1,000-watt metal halide / sodium lights in a closet. A stationary 400-watt

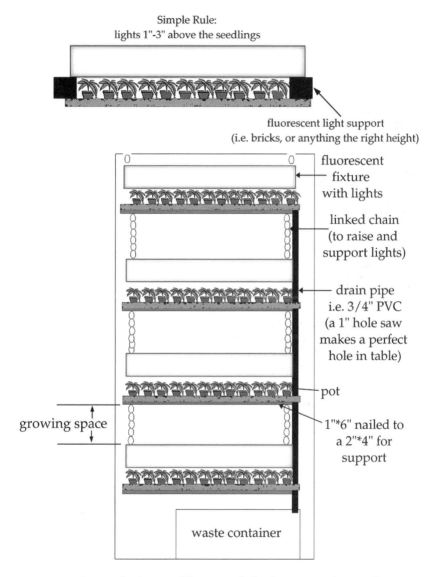

Simple Rule:
lights 1"-3" above the seedlings

fluorescent light support
(i.e. bricks, or anything the right height)

fluorescent
fixture
with lights

linked chain
(to raise and
support lights)

drain pipe
i.e. 3/4" PVC
(a 1" hole saw
makes a perfect
hole in table)

pot

growing space

1"*6" nailed to
a 2"*4" for
support

waste container

Figures 1.1 and 1.2: Multiple tiers of fluorescent lights for growing short seedlings.

bulb effectively covers up to 16 square feet of space. Using a light mover adds another one-third of usable space, resulting in about 21 square feet. A stationary 1,000-watt bulb effectively covers up to 64 square feet. A track or Sun Circle adds another one-third of usable square footage.

2. Oscillating fan.

Top left: A track or Sun Circle; Top right: smell removal system; Middle left: oscillating fan; Bottom left: exhaust fan; Bottom right: air cooling for lights.

3. Exhaust fan.

4. Air-cooling for lights (if necessary).

5. A custom gardening system for the desired space (see chapter 4).

6. Smell removal system(if necessary). Items of smell removal in the grow room are ionizers, or air neutralizing agents such as Ona. Items to remove odors in the exhaust vent are ozone generators and charcoal filters.

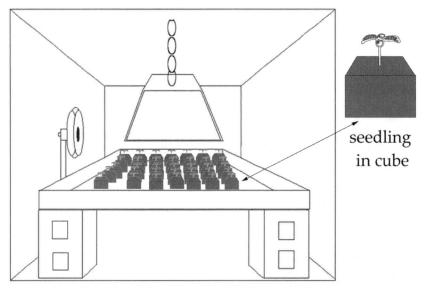

seedling
in cube

Figure 1.3: Seedlings placed under a 400-watt metal halide light.

Maintenance

It is important to maintain a proper room temperature (70 to 80°F), a proper root temperature (slightly under 70°F), and a proper humidity (40 to 70%) so that the walls will not mold and plants are in a healthy environment for optimal growth. In other words, the space may require good ventilation, air-cooled lights, and / or an air conditioner in order to acquire the proper variables for optimum or satisfactory growth, if a grower uses the more powerful 400 to 1,000-watt halide / sodium bulbs.

Air conditioner

In most cases, seedlings do not smell, but there are exceptions. For small spaces, an ionizer in the room should do the trick.

Starting Seeds

Ideally, the grower cultivates with a strain or strains that will grow well in the indoor grow room, produce a hearty yield, and have the odor and / or flavor of preference. It helps to know a seed's history. The more that is known, the less

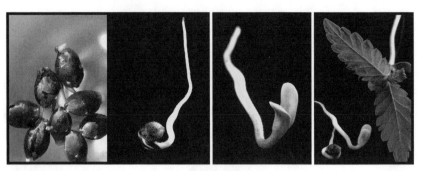

The first phases of life are shown from left to right.

the gamble. After obtaining the preferred seed stock, a grower should follow the next set of instructions in order to get off to a good start. Remember, growing one crop is at least a 3-month commitment!

A. Water should be boiled (to sterilize it), placed in a clean jar or glass, and allowed to cool to room temperature. Soaking the seeds in water for 24 to 48 hours is the next step. Then, seeds should be removed from the water and wrapped in wet cheesecloth or cotton. The seeds must not dry out. Lukewarm water can be used to remoisten the cloth.

B. Find the sprouted germinants. Some germinants may sprout right away, while others may sprout days later.

C. The germinants should be placed into a growing medium, for which there are several choices: potting soil, soilless mix, peat moss, rockwool cubes, oasis cubes, and peat pellets. Before seeds are placed in the growing medium, a small hole should be made to bury the seedling so that it lies ⅛ of an inch under the medium. In each casethe seed part should be up, and the white tail should be pointing downward. The seedling should be handled delicately when it is covered in the medium so that the stalk does not break.

    1. Sprouted seeds can be put in pots (about 4 inches high) that contain potting soil, soilless mix, or peat moss. Several germinants can be placed in one container at first, then they should be transplanted into individual containers before they start to develop too many roots. Normally, less than a week is a good time to transplant the young plants into individual contain-

Among other things, germinated seeds can go directly into soil or rockwool cubes.

ers. After a week or so, roots will tangle and the job becomes more difficult. The longer the time frame for putting a germinant in its own container, the greater the odds of stunting the plant. A spoon can be used to scoop out tiny plants so that they can be moved to individual containers.

2. Seedlings can be put in rockwool or oasis cubes, but the cubes must not dry out. If cubes dry out, plants can die or growth can be stunted.

3. Peat pellets work, too. Add water to make the cubes expand before planting the germinants.

D. The planted seedlings should be placed 1 to 3 inches beneath fluorescent lights, or 1½ to 2 feet under a 400-watt metal halide bulb.

Often, the more expensive specialty fluorescent grow tubes are worth the extra bucks. Daylight fluorescent tubes work, too. Alternating a cool white and a warm white in a fluorescent light fixture is a cheap way of making it through the seedling phase. Using only cool whites or warm whites will work, if no other tubes are available. But using only warm whites or only cool whites results in slower growth, and, some plants may turn a little yellow due to inadequate lighting.

Mice
Mice like little shoots. Therefore, they should not have access to young plants.

Seedling Care
Feeding
A fertilizing routine should be started about 10 days to a couple of weeks after

Dying leaves. This is a sign that something has gone wrong.

germination. A grower should use fertilizer only at half strength during vegetative growth. An example is to use Sea Mix 3-2-2, Alaska Fish Fertilizer, liquid kelp, or any other fertilizer at half strength.

If plants are placed on a flood table, feeding maintenance is lowered dramatically. A leakproof table can be flooded by hand, or with a pump. Chapter 4 explains how to build a flood and drain system.

Over- and underwatering can stunt a plant, which leads to poor production. Overwatering is most common in potting soil that is not allowed to drain. If the soil is saturated with water, there is little air in it. When cubes, etc. are frequently saturated with solution, the solution drains well and the roots can receive an abundance of air due to the nature of the medium.

Temperature

Seedlings can grow well in cool and warm temperatures. However, hot tempera-

Misting plants regularly with water or liquid kelp helps deter bugs.

tures can stunt plants. The ability to grow well in cool temperatures varies from strain to strain. A temperature of around 70 to 80°F is safe for most strains.

Seedlings that are severely yellow with stiff, woodlike stalks will not grow to be healthy plants; they will be stunted. The stalks should be soft and bendable.

An option is to mist the plants with a sprayer daily or every few days: leaves and stalks may look more vibrant.

Lighting

If fluorescent lights are used, each pot should be placed so that the top of the plant is 2 inches beneath the lights.

For a 400-watt halide light, the light distance can start at 1½ to 2 feet above the plants. In general, placing the lights 1½-feet above the plants is a safe distance for good growth until plants outgrow the seedling phase in 4 to 5 weeks.

Running the lights for 18-hour periods on a timer is recommended during

Timers can run all of the electrical equipment in a grow room.

the seedling stage and vegetative growth. As the plants grow, the lights should be raised so they are always at a constant distance from the plant tops.

After seedlings are 4 to 5 weeks old they can be transplanted to the indoor vegetative room that is discussed in chapter 4. This allows a grower to get a decent-sized crop. The plants can be moved out of a seedling room sooner, such as 2 to 3 weeks, but the growth rate will be slow until the plants are about 5 to 6 weeks old. Or the plants can be induced to flower under the same lights using a 12-hour on / 12-hour off photoperiod, if a grower wants a few buds from that setup.

Transplanting Seedlings

Seedlings can be transplanted into any system from pages 49 to 181. Indoor gardening systems can be put together several ways, using systems such as: soil / soilless, hydroponic, and aeroponic. For all gardening systems, there are building and maintaining references in chapters 4 and 5.

Plants can be transplanted at any time of the vegetative growth phase. As a

Looking into the future. A grower wants these healthy results; vibrant leaves and no signs of problems.

general rule, plants should be able to spread their roots and not become too root-bound. Plants should not be transplanted during flowering.

Plants can be transplanted from one medium to another. For example, plants in rockwool, clay, perlite, soilless mix, or dirt can go into any other medium. Plant roots will adapt to various root environments: the key is to feed the roots properly at all times. For example, a plant in peat moss or soilless mix that is transplanted to clay or perlite will need a new feeding program because soilless mix can be constantly irrigated or it can go days between irrigation. However, roots growing in a medium such as clay cannot go days between waterings, given that plants are being raised under a proper climate. Many

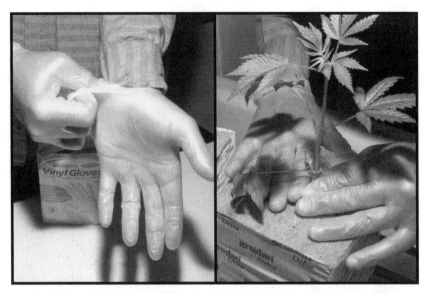

Wearing latex gloves while transplanting the plant helps to avoid contamination.

growers have rooms too hot. In that case, the roots will dry up even faster in mediums that do not hold moisture for a long time without irrigation.

Following a pattern of continuous feeding for 5 to 6 days and flushing for 1 day is the safest method for providing a healthy root environment for growing plants in all hydroponic mediums. A hydroponic grower can never go wrong if he follows this basic rule of 1 flush per week. Aeroponics can feed without flushing (until 2 weeks before harvest), using aeroponic plant food.

Sometimes a grower will start seedlings in one of many hydroponic mediums; like a small container of flat of soilless mix, peat moss, or rockwool cube because they are easy and quick to use. Plants in one of these mediums can be transplanted to soil, too. Plants that are transplanted into soil can be cared for as though they are being grown in soil. Plants should be transplanted from a hydroponic (aeroponic) medium into soil at the youngest age possible in order to prevent stress.

Roots in soil or soilless mix anchor in the medium to keep roots intact. That makes transplanting a snap, especially if mix is not too wet or too dry. A grower should always keep soilless mix somewhere between too dry and too wet if feeding is done periodically (i.e. once a week). However, plants grown in soilless mix that are continuously fed with a top-feeding hydroponic system will grow faster than plants that are fed or watered periodically in soilless mix.

Systematically, small plants are moved into larger pots.

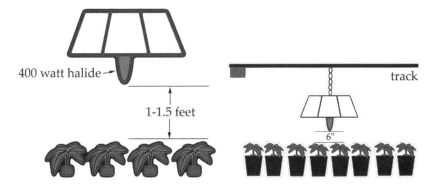

Figures 1.4 and 1.5: Distance specifications for stationary and mobile 400-watt lights.

These budding plants under a sun circle have spent their entire life in rockwool cubes.

Spacing

Seedlings can be spaced far from each other and left to grow together, or they can be put closer together and trained away from each other. A grower should use 1 to 3 seedlings per 2 to 5-gallon bucket.

Bulb Placement

When stationary bulbs are used, young seedlings should be placed 1¹/₂-feet under a 400-watt metal halide bulb or 2-feet under a 1,000-watt metal halide bulb for the first week. Then, they should be placed at a distance of 1 to 1¹/₂-feet under the bulbs for the duration of the vegetative process. Another option is to place the marijuana plants within 6 to 8 inches of the light if a track or a Sun Circle is used. If air- or water-cooled lights are used during flowering, the plants can be placed within inches of the bulbs. (See Figures 1.4 and 1.5)

What a Grower Should Know about Seedlings

Marijuana plants are male, female, or hermaphrodites. When a grower knows the difference, he can make the garden grow more efficiently, especially if seed-

These plants grow in traditional pots filled with soilless mix.

less flowers are desired. Pulling plants with male pollen (males and hermaphrodites) allows for the production of seedless flowers. In order to make seeds, identifying and using pollen immediately (or storing immediately in the freezer) is the key, especially for the serious breeder. (Breeding is explained in detail in chapter 7.)

Sexing Seedlings

Some growers can identify the sex of plant seeds. A trick to sexing plants that are 3 to 5 weeks old is to decrease the photoperiod from 18 down to 12 hours. When the lights run at 12 hours for 3 to 5 days, the plants' flowering mechanisms are triggered. After the 3 to 5 days, the light timer should be reset to run for 18 hours. Males show soon by forming pollen sacks, and females normally show soon afterward with pistils. Sometimes, a female will show pistils sooner than a male shows pollen sacks.

Putting Seedlings to the Test

Putting young seedlings through tests such as over-watering, under-watering, drought, high heat, low light, cramped spacing, etc. can help sort out the strong plants from the weak plants. However, just because plants look best at a young age does not mean that they will necessarily demonstrate the ability to out-produce those that were shocked or died at a young age due to adverse conditions. Nevertheless, on the whole, plants that are strong tend to continue being strong plants through adulthood.

If many seeds are started in one small container, they should be trans-

At this time, plants should be spaced and separated when the leaves touch each other.

planted into individual containers no later than when they are 2 weeks old to prevent shock and stunting. The 2-week-old plants need to be carefully separated at the roots without bending the stalks or pulling out pieces of roots before the transplanting process or some plants may get stunted. Plants can be buried up to the first set of leaves.

2

Growing with Clones

Cloning is fairly easy and should be done when plants are in vegetative growth. Cloning involves taking a piece of a known mother plant and creating other plants with the same genetic makeup. A mother plant should be a vigorous, healthy female plant with plenty of shoots to take cuttings from.

When clones are taken in vegetative growth and rooted, they will grow quickly right off the bat. This is a good habit to get into for cutting clones.

Clones taken from plants that don't show any buds (i.e. 2 weeks into flowering) may produce small buds during the 18-hour rooting photoperiod. However, they rejuvenate into vegetative growth rather quickly when they are

Cuttings rooting in 1-inch rockwool cubes.

Top view of plant in vegetative growth which is suitable for cutting clones.

Heat pad warms the cubes during rooting.

put in a vegetative light cycle or long daylight days after they form roots.

Plants that are cloned during the flowering process (when buds are noticeable) will take longer to revert into fast vegetative growth, and time is lost. Sometimes, depending on factors such as the strain, plants will not revert to healthy vegetative growth. This means that plants will take on a permanent 1 to 4 leaf growth pattern, and they will not be as compact as if they had a regular leaf pattern of 5, 7, or 9 leaves. The plants will be far less productive than clones taken during vegetative growth.

The stage of the budding process at which the clones are taken has a big impact on the quality of the new cutting's growth. Clones taken toward the end of the budding process have more potential problems than those taken earlier in the flowering process. Checking leaf texture also helps in determining plant quality. If the leaves of the new cuttings become waxy and stiff, unlike normal soft and flexible growth, then problems can be expected. These plants with the waxy material should be pulled, because they will be unproductive. Plants with an abnormal leaf pattern but normal-textured leaves will probably rejuvenate to become productive.

Plants that Are Started from Seed

When seed is used for growing indoors, a grower has the option of cutting female clones when the plant's sex is determined. The female sex can be determined by finding pistils growing from the nodes (stalk and branch intersections). Looking for early flower formations is advised, too. Plants with the pistils should not have male pollen sacks along the stalks. Those plants that have both pollen and pistils are hermaphrodites, and these plants can make an unknown quantity of seed. Hermaphroditism can creep in at any time, although it occurs very rarely, especially in a quality garden.

No

Cloning Supplies

1. 10x20-inch tray and matching propagation lid (7 inches high). Available at garden centers and hydroponic shops.

2. Propagation mat or heat pad. Mat available at hydroponic shops; pad at drugstores.

3. Thirty or more 1½-inch oasis propagation cubes, rockwool cubes or small plastic cutting containers. Available at hydroponic shops or garden centers.

4. Vitamin B1: 1.7oz (50ml).

5. Rooting hormone.

6. Fluorescent light fixture with bulbs.

7. Timer (optional).

Cloning Procedure

A. From 4 to 6 shoots should be left above the spot where the cut is made. This is a critical step. The new cutting-to-be will have about 3 shoots at the top and 2 more down the stalk.

B. The next step is removing 2 bottom side shoots. Different strains will have different growth patterns of the spaces between the node intersections. It is best to have a cutting in which both cut nodes can fit into the rooting medium.

Typical cutting in a 1-inch cube.

A mixture is prepared for soaking the cubes.

C. The cut nodes should be placed in a jar of water. This procedure is repeated until the desired number of cuttings has been taken. It is better for a novice to take only a few cuttings at a time, so that the learning curve will be faster. There is no point in taking 30 cuttings, only to find that one mistake, such as drying out the rooting medium, ruined the whole batch.

D. The next step is soaking organic oasis-cubes, rockwool cubes, or cutting containers with organic soilless mix. Sunshine Mix is a popular soilless mix. Oasis cubes and rockwool are simpler for the novice. A recommended organic method is soaking rooting medium in a liquid mixture: ½ the recommended strength of liquid kelp and a few drops of vitamin B1 in 1 gallon of water is a safe formula. Alternatively, a few drops of vitamin B1 works well in water. Some people use plain water and get high survival.

Sheets of rockwool cubes or oasis cubes can be soaked in a typical 10x20-inch nursery flat that fits 96 cubes perfectly. After the soaking, they can be placed into another clean flat.

E. Excess water should be squeezed out of the growing medium; too much water and the rooting process becomes slower. If the rooting medium is too dry, the cuttings will wilt and die. Wet, but not too wet, is the way to get decent results. Some say that

The future. Rooted clones moved into a new growing system. The plastic keeps the roots free of light.

if the rooting medium is not too wet, the cuttings form new roots more quickly, because the plant will tend to seek out water by spreading its roots. However, this is a fine line, because too little water will lower the cuttings' chances of survival. .

F. A nail can be used to make holes in the cubes or growing mix, if no holes are present. The hole should not go all of the way through the cloning medium. The two side-shoot nodes should be covered by the cloning medium without the stem going through the bottom.

G. The bottom two nodes of the cutting are dipped into a rooting hormone, then, placed in the cubes or containers. This procedure is repeated for all cuttings. If the distances between the cut nodes are too far apart to be covered by the rooting cubes, then an option is to stack a cube on top of another cube. If

Clone turned to gold.

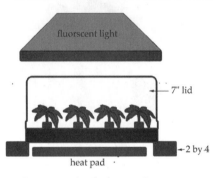

Figure 2.1: Simple, low-maintenance cloning setup.

soilless mix or perlite / vermiculite is being used, then a deeper container will solve the depth problem.

H. The clones are then placed in a tray and covered with the lid (a piece of clear, raised plastic designed to fit the tray). The tray can be placed on a propagating mat or one inch above a heating pad, especially if the clones are rooting in a cold area. Clones will root faster when the roots receive proper heat (approximately 70°F). If clones are rooting at room temperature, the roots in the medium will be cooler than room temperature.

I. The fluorescent fixture should be placed 2 to 4 inches above the dome to supply adequate lighting during rooting. The lights should be set on a timer to run for 18 hours a day. However, rooting clones under a 24-hour photoperiod does the trick for a skinny budget. Nevertheless, it is a good idea to give the plants a 6-hour rest. It is natural for plants to take a rest, and they will do different things in the dark.

Maintenance

The plastic lid cannot have any cracks or warps because clones could dry up and die overnight, especially babied clones from a weak strain. The ruggedness of a strain is a major factor.

Some growers mist several times a day. This can give better results. Sometimes, lids retain a lot of moisture; sometimes, the moisture escapes easily from under the lid.

Roots may start growing out of the bottoms and sides of the cubes within

1 to 4 weeks. The time length varies from strain to strain.

Periodically adding small amounts of plain water to the cubes or mix is a good idea, especially if the medium seems to get a little dry. Remember, over-soaking is wrong and is not going to help matters. Overwatering slows down the rooting process and can cause stem rot. Overwatered clones that do make it are often weak and may not form a strong plant.

Roots growing out of medium.

Some growers don't mist at all, leave their cuttings fully exposed to the air, and yet get decent results, believing that only the strong survive. However, this method causes the roots to use up a lot of water. Therefore, frequent watering to the roots is a must when moistening the roots with this method, or, keeping the roots sitting in a shallow solution of water / nutrient solution. Air to the roots is less available from constant liquid saturation. If the rooting medium sits in a solution full time, the cuttings will root slowly, and the new roots will be skinny. The clones will look weaker than those that are in moist cubes in a dry cloning tray with a lid. Therefore, sitting roots in solution is not recommended.

Transplanting Clones

As soon as roots show from the cubes or mix, the clones should be transplanted into the desired bucket, ideally 5-gallon containers.

Sometimes, if several clones are started at the same time, some may seem to root, while others look weak or dying. Weak-looking cuttings can be given a little tug so that a grower knows which cuttings are rooting and which ones aren't. The cuttings that resist have anchoring roots, while the really weak or dying clones will come out easily. The rooting time can vary from strain to strain.

Transplanting Procedure

Plants can be transplanted at any time of the vegetative growth phase. As a gen-

Rooted cubes can go into any medium, such as the soilless mix in pots shown above.

eral rule, plants should be able to spread their roots and not become too root-bound. Plants should not be transplanted during flowering.

Plants can be transplanted from one medium to another. For example, plants in rockwool, clay, perlite, soilless mix, dirt, etc., can go into any other medium.

Plant roots will adapt to various root environments. The key is to feed the roots properly at all times. For example, a plant in peat moss or soilless mix that is transplanted to clay, perlite, etc., will need a new feeding program, because soilless

Clones in cubes can go into an aggregate medium like lava rock and clay pellets.

mix can be constantly irrigated or it can go days between irrigation. However, roots located in a medium such as clay, cannot go days between waterings, given that plants are grown under a strong climate. The same holds true if a plant is transplanted from a medium like rockwool or clay, into soil or soilless mix.

Roots in soil or soilless mix anchor in the medium to keep roots intact. That makes transplanting a snap, especially if mix is not too wet, nor too dry. Anyhow, a grower should always keep soilless mix somewhere between too dry and too wet.

1-inch rockwool cube transplanted into 3-inch rockwool cube.

Cloning Notes
Growing Larger Plants with Two Rooms

Cutting clones for 2-room indoor growing soon before plants go into the bud room maximizes bud room space and creates a smooth cycle. If new clones are cut from a mother plant in the vegetative room immediately before the plants in the bud room finish budding, they will root and be ready to transplant into the vegetative room at the same time the veg room plants are ready to go into the flower room.

This is the ideal cycle: plants out of the bud room for harvesting, and new plants from the vegetative room into the bud room right away. At the same time, new clones are put into the vegetative room. The next clones are taken when the estimated rooting time corresponds with the next harvest.

3

Building an Indoor Grow Room

The vegetative room is where the young clones or seedlings will begin as tiny plants and eventually grow into robust plants before they start the flowering process. The sex of a marijuana plant is either male, female, or hermaphrodite. The flower-producing females are the desired producers of bud.

Pot plants from seed can be started under fluorescent lights for the first 4 to 6 weeks after germination because most strains grow well from seed for 3 to 6 weeks under this type of light without any problems. This is the first stage, before the seedlings receive the metal halide light treatment in the full vegetative room setup. (Seedlings are discussed in depth in chapter 1.)

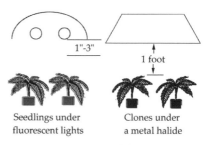

Seedlings under fluorescent lights

Clones under a metal halide

Figure 3.1: Distance guidelines for fluorescent and halide lights.

Clones can go directly under the metal halide light(s) when they have made roots, as discussed in chapter 2.

Grow Room Supplies and Building Materials

All the materials in the following list are designed for grow rooms of any size. The rules are basic in order to calculate the equipment needed for any size room. All the information regarding the proper gear is explained below under vegetative / flower room setup.

Proper lighting and distance creates quality bud.

1. Lights and hoods
Important Rules of Vegetative Room Lighting
A stationary 400-watt bulb effectively covers up to 16 square feet of space. Using a light mover adds another one-third of usable space, resulting in about 21 square feet. A stationary 1,000-watt bulb effectively covers up to 64 square feet. A track or Sun Circle adds another one-third of usable square footage. Ideally, the ceiling height is between 7 and 10 feet. A 95-watt Envirolite covers 2.6 square feet.

Left: pH control for quality feeding is important, as is a quality grow room.
Right: Getting to the full flower stage is a commitment of time.

There are many different qualities of metal halide and sodium lights on the market. It is recommended that a grower ask about the life of a bulb at the time of purchase. Light meters can be used to determine light quality, too.

Bulbs should be washed with a citrus cleanser like TKO between crops to remove dust, bugs, and mist residue.

There is more information about lights and lighting accessories on pages 209 to 215.

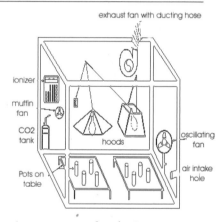

Figure 3.2: Set up for a basic grow room.

2. Thermometer / humidistat or high-tech climate controller.

3. Squirrel or in-line exhaust fan (265cfm [cubic feet per minute] or more) will be adequate for rooms up to 12x12-feet.

4. Oscillating fan, 12 to 18 inches.

5. One heavy-duty grounded timer.

6. Hooks to suspend the lights.

7. Linked chain for hanging the lamps.

8. Reflective material: flat white latex, alumicool, white plastic, or reflective Mylar for wall reflection. Mylar is expensive, while alumicool is moderately cheap.

9. One-gallon pump sprayer.

10. Proper size vacuum hose (i.e. 5 to 6 inches) for exhaust fan (approximately 10-feet will be required).

11. pH pens for liquid (optional, but highly recommended).

12. pH buffer 7 solution (optional).

13. One-arm or two-arm Sun Circle for one or two lights, or track for one or two lights (optional).

14. Fire extinguisher.

15. Grounded adapter to modify timer to three outlets when running the 18-hour equipment.

A timer board can also be used to run a larger system using more lights, such as 240-volt. Available from electrical shops and hydroponic stores.

Vegetative / Flower Room Setup

The room circuit should check in with at least 15 amps. Circuit checks can be done by leaving a stereo on while flipping the main breaker switches off and on. When the stereo shuts down, a grower should read the amperage on the switch at the main breaker. The stereo can be plugged into other circuits to see which other wall outlets are running on the same breaker.

Regular household circuits run on 120 volts, with the 240-volt exception of dryers and ovens.

Watts = volts x amps

Amps = watts ÷ volts

For example, with a 1,000-watt light running on a 120-volt circuit:

1,000 watts ÷ 120 volts = 9.1 amps

This leaves about 4 more amps as a margin of safety on a 15-amp circuit. Equipment normally uses more amps than a formula indicates, so it is a good idea to allow 10 to 15% unused amperage, to max out the circuit. If too many amps are used on one circuit, a fuse will blow, and all gear on the circuit will shut down.

A. The room should be cleaned and disinfected because a dirty or moldy room invites bug or mildew problems, which can lead to plant stress and disease, all of which affect yields.

B. The walls should be painted with flat white latex or covered with reflective

Small, budding plants under illumination.

Mylar, white plastic, or alumicool. Reflective material is important because light will hit the walls and reflect back, adding more usable light to the plants, which means greater yields. Alumicool, white plastic, and paint are fairly cheap options that work well. Paint is permanent, while alumicool and white plastic are user-friendly and easy to use over and over again should the room be torn down. Mylar reflects best, but it costs the most and must be handled very carefully, for it crinkles easily and, as a result, loses its reflective ability.

C. A place should be found in a high space, such as the attic or fireplace, for air to exhaust with an exhaust fan. A grower can go without an exhaust fan, but the plants will be weaker and grow slower than they will in a room with quality air. As a result of an insufficient climate, plants are often less healthy, and that invites predators such as spider mites to take advantage of the weak plants. Air ventilation is extremely important so that CO_2 can be replenished from the outside environment, to avoid stagnant air problems. Plants respond much better to a higher air quality.

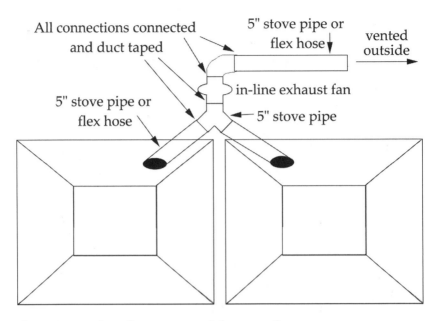

Figure 3.3: One exhaust fan can remove air from more than one room.

Inserting an Exhaust Fan

A proper-sized hole should be cut with a jigsaw for the vacuum hose and / or stovepipe to go through. (Figure 3.3) This job is easy if the pipe can be placed in a straight line to a vent on the side of the house with little distance to travel. Some growers just vent the air into the attic without sending it directly outdoors. This helps the plants get decent air, but this method can leave a mess behind for the homeowner if excessive humidity is continually sent into this space without care. Molds and mildew can thrive in moist areas, leaving black, greasy stains behind. However, there are mold removers on the market. Stovepipe is cheap, comes in a variety of sizes, and can be directed to various locations via flexible elbows that connect the sections of the metal stovepipe. Vacuum hose, on the other hand, has the best flexibility for awkward locations. The two can be used together and this is often a good match because pipe is sturdier, while the vacuum hose offers needed flexibility.

If a squirrel fan is used, it should be suspended from two hooks screwed into the ceiling, or hung with a coat hanger. Duct tape is handy for connecting the exhaust fan to the hose.

If an in-line fan is used for exhausting, it can be mounted inside or outside the room, because hose can be attached to both ends. The advantages of an in-line fan are that it is quiet and an adapter can be attached at one end so air can be sucked from more than one room at a time. Adding pipe or hose on the end of an in-line fan helps keep the noise down. Fans will be most effective when the air travels in a straight line. Fortunately, some in-line fans have more torque than others and therefore can push air effectively even when air is not moved in a straight line.

Purchasing an Exhaust Fan

The room volume can be calculated by multiplying length x width x height. For example, a room may be 10 feet long, 10 feet wide, and 8 feet high, to give 800 cubic feet. Exhaust fans will remove so many cubic feet per minute (cfm). If an exhaust fan can remove 800 cubic feet (the room's volume) in 1 to 5 minutes, it will do fine. In this case, a 265-cfm fan will remove all the air from a room in about 3 minutes:

265 cfm x 3 minutes = 795 cubic feet

A fan of this size is recommended for rooms from 265 to 1,325 cubic feet.

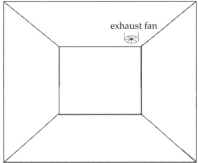

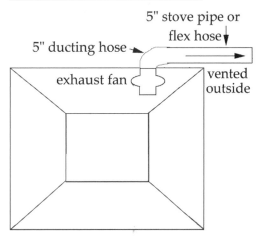

Figures 3.4 through 3.6: Steps for inserting an exhaust fan and hose.

Smell Removal

A device to remove smell can be inserted into the exhaust pipe after the exhaust fan. Boxes with charcoal filters or ozone generators can be used to zap unwanted skunklike odors before they are sent outside. There are ready-made products, such as Magic Dragon and

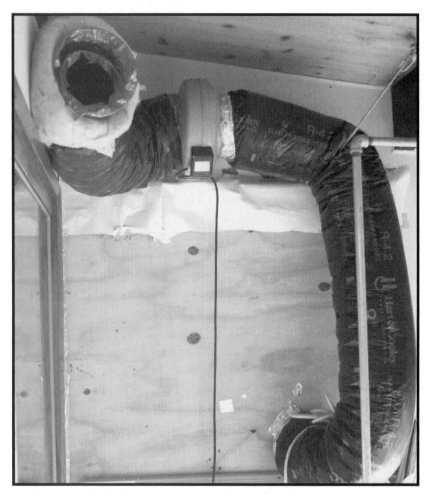

Flex hose is attached to fan to remove air to a desired location.

Uvonair that can be inserted easily into exhaust pipes. (Figure 3.7)

The proper ionizer may remove odors inside of the room, and it removes pollen that may make more seeds than desired. An ionizer can be used in an enclosed room or a room where is exhausted outside of the grow room. However, if the air is not sent outside, carbon dioxide enrichment is a must so that the air does not get stagnant.

An air conditioner can be used to cool a room and exhaust the air into another location. In this case, a charcoal filter can be used to eliminate odors inside of a grow room without sending the air running through the filter out-

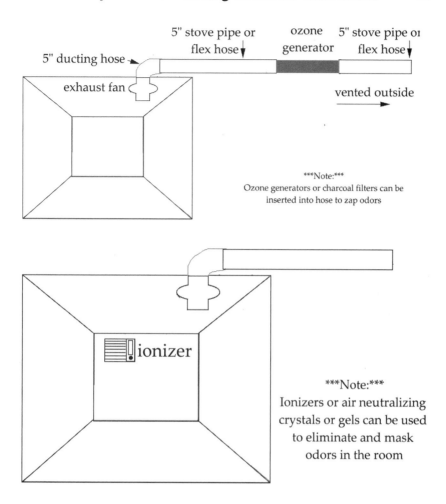

Figure 3.7 and 3.8: Options for smell removal.

side. This is a popular set-up for trailer gardens that fit into garages, warehouses, and outside. The trailers are mobile and discreet.

Some strains are almost 100% odor free while growing, while others will smell like a stinky skunk. It is up to the grower to figure out what combination of smell removers will work best under a given condition. If the odor factor is not dealt with, the penalty can be harsh.

D. Besides air exhaust, air intake is a must. A small hole (low in room and diagonal to the exhaust fan), about 6 inches in diameter, directed into another cool

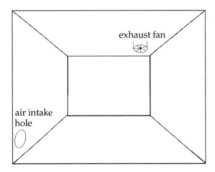 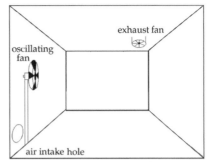

Figure 3.9 and 3.10: Air intake hole, exhaust fan, and oscillating fan all contribute to air quality.

room will do, although adding an air intake fan to bring fresh air from outside via ducting or vacuum hose would allow for fresher air. For extra air quality, a filter, such as an ionizer, may also be added to keep particulate from entering the room.

E. An oscillating fan should be placed in the corner of the room to circulate air by pushing it away from the fan. Air movement is important to stir up the air and bring windlike conditions resembling those of the great outdoors. Blowing air under the bulbs helps to avoid burning of top shoots if the lights happen to get close to the plants. Air-cooled lights are a good option for bulbs.

Lights and Garden System Setup

The gardening system and lights can be set up at the same time because they will make a custom match, but before the lights are set up, the grower should decide which type of gardening system is going to be used. A grower will choose between a "flat garden," "V-system," or "column system." Flat gardens can be used to grow plants of all sizes, but V-systems and column systems are used to grow small plants for the top buds. How to build each system will be described below, and I will include appropriate lighting strategies. Basic to every setup is having a system with sufficient lighting and the proper plant supply. If one crop is grown, a grower can acquire clones, make clones, or use seedlings to get the proper plant supply.

The hooks are screwed into the ceiling studs. To locate the 2x6 or 2x4 stud, tapping the ceiling and listening for a strong, dull sound or using a stud sensor will locate it. The linked chain will be hung on the hook(s) to suspend the light kit(s). The area should be covered effectively, using the following rules for light placement. Plywood sheets or 2x4s can be nailed to the ceiling to support lights in the desired spot.

The next section covers the three possible systems that can be used: flat garden, V-system, or column system.

Flat Garden

A flat garden is a garden for which the plants are all at the same level, such as on the floor. (Figure 3.11) The flat garden could be a simple dirt garden or an elaborate hydroponic system. Here is a list of building plans and maintenance for flat garden systems. They are listed from easiest to hardest.

Flat Garden Systems
1. Billy Bob's Organic Hydroponic System, p. 150
2. Soilless Mix Improvisation, p. 175
3. Soil, p. 179
4. Wick System, p. 54
5. Flood and Drain, p. 49
6. Top-Feeding Bucket System, p. 66
7. PVC Pipe Systems; NFT, p. 116; top feed, p. 86; aero, p. 129

Single Crop

The easiest way to grow a flat garden is to grow midsize or large plants because they do not require too many plants and a grower can use all of the space from floor to ceiling.

Continual Crops

Billy Bob's System on page 150, Wick System #1, Flood and Drain System on page 49, and Top-feeding buckets on page 66 explain easy ways to get continual crops in a flat garden.

Using flood tables is the easiest way to mass-produce seedlings for all growing systems: dirt, hydroponic, and aeroponic. For example, one standard

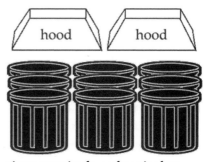

Figure 3.11: Simple garden: nine large plants under two lights.

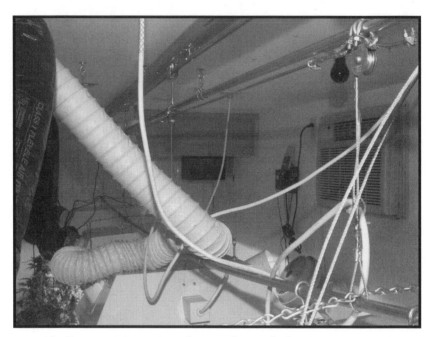

To avoid a disaster, equipment must be secured in a safe place.

4x8-foot flood table with 2,200-watt compact fluorescent lights or 1,400-watt halide with track could be used to grow 288 seedlings for five weeks before they can be transplanted. A 4x4-foot table and a 200-watt compact fluorescent or 1,400-watt halide could be used to start 144 seedlings until they are transplanted at 4 to 5 weeks old. A standard cloning flat can be used to root 96 clones; 2 flats fit under one 2-tube 4-foot fluorescent light fixture.

Important Rules of Vegetative Room Lighting

A stationary 400-watt bulb effectively covers up to 16 square feet of space. Using a light mover adds another ⅓ of usable space, resulting in about 21 square feet. A stationary 1,000-watt bulb effectively covers up to 64 square feet. A track or Sun Circle adds another ⅓ of usable square footage. Ideally, the ceiling height is between 7 to 10 feet. Figures 5.16 and 5.14 on page 213 in this chapter show a track and a circular mover like the Sun Circle. Many systems in this guide show light movers. Lights should run for 18 hours, with 6 hours of darkness.

If a Sun Circle is used, it should be placed in the middle of the room. The Sun Circle can move from 1 to 3 lights slowly around in a circle so that overhead lighting can cover an area effectively and bulbs can be positioned close to the plant tops. The Sun Circle is best used in a circular or square room.

If one track is used for the 1,000-watt halide, the best placement is in the middle of the room. Using an extension works well to make the track travel further. If one track is used for two 400-watt halides, the lights can be moved further apart as the plants get larger. Using a track allows the lightbulbs to get within inches of the plant tops. Tracks are advantageous when used in a rectangular room, because they move back and forth in a straight line.

Patience is necessary when wiring all light-moving gear together, especially the Sun Circle.

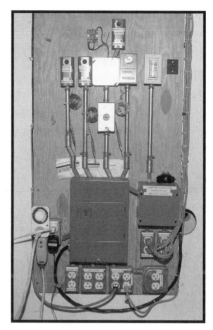

Advanced wiring techniques provide many usable outlets.

The safety box with the ballast and capacitor should be placed on insulation board on top of a brick or cement block. These materials can absorb the heat produced from a ballast. The ballast and capacitor could be placed in another room to keep the room temperature down, or placed somewhere a little heat is needed, such as a cool corner near an air-intake vent. The ballast can be hung with a sturdy coat hanger, or it can be surrounded with cinder blocks to keep down the humming noise.

Warning: Rubber shoes should always be worn in the room, because accidentally touching the capacitor connections with wet hands can send an unforgettable shock through the body.

Important Flower Room Rule

For every 4 to 25 square feet in the flower room, a 400-watt sodium or halide can be used for the light source. For every 16 to 64 square feet in the flower room, a 1,000-watt sodium or halide can be used. More light per square foot will give more productive results during budding if the climate is proper. These light-per-square-footage ranges are the high and low ends of the production scale and will affect crop yield if all other variables, such as proper airflow and fertilization, are met. Staying within these ranges is advised.

To keep it simple, the light kits should be plugged into a timer(s) set for 12 hours for the entire flowering process. Marijuana is a short day flowering plant that needs about 12 hours to produce the flowers. However, the time can be adjusted for the serious grower, such as using 13 hours of light for flowering with a particular strain, or using 10 hours at the end of the flowering process.

Lights may have to go into separate outlets, depending on the circuit amperage. A 1,000-watt, 400-watt kit and an oscillating fan will normally max out a regular household 15-amp circuit and an 1,875-watt timer. Regular household circuits in the U.S. and Canada run on 120 volts. Dryer and ovens run on 240 volts.

It is important to note that an old circuit in an old home may work fine for days at a time, then for whatever weird reason suddenly blow. These circuits are probably made with old wiring that is not up to code. Another possibility is that the circuit is shared with another suite in the building, and another tenant's blow-dryer is causing the problem.

To bring electricity to a desired location, one option is to extend household wire to make another outlet; another is to use 10 to 12-gauge extension cord from another outlet. Using a 14-gauge or higher extension cord results in loss of voltage, especially if the electricity travels far distances. A 10-gauge extension cord will not have a voltage drop over 100 feet.

The small light timers that run only up to 1,875 watts cannot run two 1,000-watt light kits, even if the power is there. However, using two small timers (set exactly the same) in separate circuits of regular household current is effective, but the timers should be checked periodically to make sure that they go on and off at roughly the same time.

Using a dryer or oven circuit and having the light ballasts set for 240 volts would easily run all these lights in the bud room and more, but this requires a special timer from a hydroponic shop to run them all. Changing voltages on the ballasts is simple. The wire with the volt reading is disconnected, e.g., 120 volts, and one of the other wires at the ballast and the 240-volt wire is connected in its place. The ballast will have a series of wires, 2 will say common (or com), and the others will have voltage readings, like 120v and 240v. Since one of the voltage

Sophisticated flower room setup with plants growing in rockwool.

wires will be connected (or the light will not work), it is easy to find that wire connected to electrical cord. That wire connected to the cord can be disconnected and the 240v wire can be connected in its place. Normally wire nuts are used to connect the wires or cap the unused wires with voltage readings. In the worst case scenario, electrical tape is used to keep the wires connected. Since several lights can be used in a 240-volt outlet, growers tend to plug the lights into a metal box that has several outlets and the right plug for the outlet.

In a typical grow room that runs lights on a 240-volt circuit, only the lights will run on the different voltage; while the other grow room equipment will run in standard 120-volt household circuits.

V-System

A V-system is a garden in which the plants are stacked in a V-shape to cover more space than a flat garden. The V-system could be a simple dirt garden or an

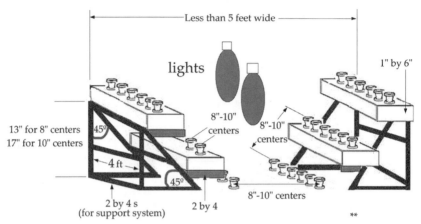

Figure 3.16 a: Simple, productive V system with traditional dirt pots.

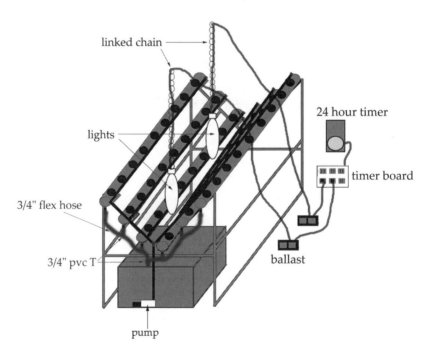

Figure 3.16 b: V system made with PVC pipe.

elaborate hydroponic system. (Figure 3.12) Here is a list of the building plans and maintenance for V-systems, listed from easiest to hardest: NFT, p.121; top-feeding, p.86; aeroponic, p.135.

Single Crop

Growing one crop requires using the correct amount of plants for the system. A grower can acquire clones for the systems or make more clones, start seeds and clone the females, or use seedlings from start to finish.

Continual Crops

If a grower uses a V-system, plants can be acquired from another room that can produce a sufficient amount of clones or seedlings. All plants can be transplanted at the same time or at different stages of growth. For example, two 6-pipe V-systems for a bedroom will need 120 clones or 120 female seedlings if they are transplanted at once.

It is possible to make over 100 clones every 7 to 10 days with two 6-pipe V-systems. Over the course of a 6-week crop, this system could make 400 or more clones, which is enough clones for 6 to 8 6-pipe V-systems.

Clones

A grower could keep a few mother plants, like 4 females, alive under a couple of 400-watt halides. Every week, every 2 weeks, or every complete harvest new clones can be transplanted into the pipes.

Plants that are in vegetative growth in a hydroponic system will grow much faster than plants that get fed every few days in dirt. A flood and drain system is the easiest way to grow mother plants for cuttings.

If a grower has space, 1 V-system could supply clones to 2 identical V-systems every week or two.

Seedlings

Five 4-foot fluorescent fixtures with female seedlings could provide this number at one time. A grower could use fluorescent fixtures with plants that are all 1 week different in age. At 5 weeks old, they can be transplanted into the pipes. Every week, 20 plants could be transplanted into the pipes to get a weekly harvest.

Close up of new transplants in rockwool cubes.

Column System

A column system is a garden in which the plants are placed in a circle around two or more bulbs. (Figure 3.14) Here is a list of the systems with building plans and maintenance instructions from easiest to most sophisticated: hand-feed, p. 94; top-feed #1, p. 97; plastic sacks, p. 112; top-feed #2, p. 105; aeroponic, p. 142.

Single Crop

Growing one crop requires using the correct amount of plants for the system. A grower can acquire clones for the systems or make more clones, start seeds and clone the females, or use seeds.

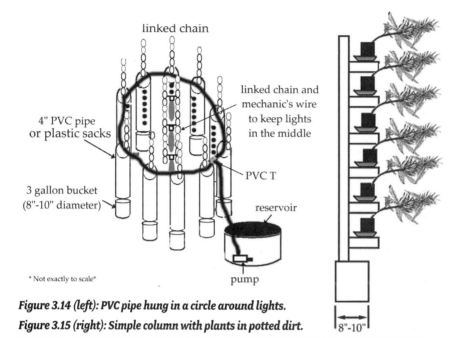

Figure 3.14 (left): PVC pipe hung in a circle around lights.
Figure 3.15 (right): Simple column with plants in potted dirt.

Continual Crops

If a grower uses a column system, plants can be acquired from another room that can produce sufficient amount of clones or seedlings. All plants can be transplanted at the same time or at different stages of growth. For example, one 12-pipe column system in a bedroom could use 72 to 100 clones or 72 to 100 female seedlings at one time if they are transplanted at once; 72 plants for the pipes, 28 plants for the floor.

It is possible to make over 100 clones every 7 to 10 days with one 12-pipe column system. Over the course of a 6-week crop, this system could make 400 or more clones, which is enough clones for 4 more column systems.

Clones

A grower could keep a few mother plants (e.g. 4 to 16) alive under a 1,000 to 2,400-watt halides in a flat garden consisting of 5 to 7-gallon pots. 4 to 8 plants would be plenty for continual harvesting while 8 to 16 should be plenty to get clones for a complete set-up. Every week, every 2 weeks, or every complete harvest new clones can be transplanted into the pipes. If a grower cuts 12 clones a week, or 24 clones every 2 weeks, he can keep a 72 plant system full of plants and

This rockwool garden will produce a flat carpet of bud.

harvest every week or two. Four plants is plenty to get 24 clones every 2 weeks .

If a grower has space, one V-system could supply clones to 2 identical V-systems every week or two.

Seedlings

Four 4-foot fluorescent fixtures with female seedlings could provide plants for a 72-plant column system at one time. A grower could use fluorescent fixtures with plants that are all 1 week different in age. At 5 weeks old, they can be transplanted into the pipes. Every week, 12 plants could be transplanted into the pipes to get a weekly harvest.

Starting the Equipment

The next step is to set one of the timers for 18 hours. A standard grounded household timer can handle 1,875-watts of power.

Next, the grounded adapter (i.e. the power bar) should be plugged into the

Left: A fire extinguisher is a necessary safety measure. Right: Kind flowers can be obtained if the growing variables are adequate.

timer. The lights and oscillating fan should also be plugged into that adapter. The timer is plugged into the wall. If more lights are used that would exceed the 1,875 watts, then a different timer that can run several lights at once is recommended. If a grower is running several lights, such as 3 to 8, it is best to use a 240-volt dryer or oven circuit because that circuit can handle more amperage. With a more powerful timer purchased from a hydroponic store, more lights can be hooked up to one circuit if they are running on a 240-volt circuit. The oscillating fan can be programmed to give intermittent cool breezes throughout the hours of darkness or it can run full-time.

The exhaust fan should be plugged into a separate outlet and left on. Things have now begun.

All lights and power-consuming gadgets in the vegetative room can run effectively on one standard 15-amp household circuit, if excessive power is not being used by other items. However, rooms larger than the size of common bedrooms will use more juice (electricity), since more lights will be used.

A fire extinguisher should be placed in an easily accessible location, because faulty household wiring and faulty ballast wiring have the potential to start a fire.

Transplanting

Now, the plants (clones and / or seedlings) can be transplanted into the growing system of choice, for example the organic hydroponic technique discussed later on in this chapter. It's more productive to grow marijuana plants from cuttings, since the females, not the males, produce the desired flowers, and this way you can be assured of having female plants.

Clones: A clone may now be transplanted into the mix of each container. Clones are cuttings of plants taken from a mother plant. The clone will be genetically similar to the mother plant. Besides assuring female plants, clones are more productive because they grow quickly after they have formed roots, and they are "knowns," unlike some seeds, which have scattered genetics and unpredictable growth cycles. A grower can buy clones or grow his own mother plant for his cuttings. Chapter 2 explains cloning procedures and other facts regarding clones.

Seedlings: To transplant seedlings, 1 to 3 seedlings should be placed in each bucket at equal distances from each other and from the sides of the container, in a triangular pattern. One plant may do for a strain that grows large, but more may be needed for varieties that produce more volume. A grower can use female seeds or 0sex regular seeds that will have males and females. Sexing is described on page 15. Chapter 1 has more detailed instructions about starting plants from seed. Female seeds or sexing seedlings of a pure strain will be the most predictable way to use seedlings.

There are major disadvantages when seedlings are used to grow marijuana plants. One problem is that they take about 5 weeks to outgrow the seedling phase to the point where they will put on quick mass similar to that of a newly rooted clone. Another setback is that seedlings might be males that do not produce the flowers, and that brings waste into the program as well as the chance of producing a seed crop rather than the desired seedless flowers.

4

Hydroponic and Organic Systems

Building a Flood and Drain System

Materials (for each flood table)

1. Flood table made to size or plastic store-bought model.
2. Two ½-inch poly elbows.
3. Two ½-inch poly Ts.
4. One role of ½-inch poly tubing.
5. Two ¾-inch thru-hull fittings.
6. One reservoir (should hold about 12 gallons of fertilized solution per each 4x4 table space).
7. Plastic covering for tray, or a growing medium such as perlite, perlite / vermiculite, coco fibers / perlite, or expanded clay.
8. Pump (250 to 350 mag drive for 4x4 to 12x12-foot space. Stronger pumps can be used for larger tables).
9. Panty hose to cover pump (optional).
10. ¾-inch plywood to support table.
11. Four sawhorse hinges per table
12. Eight pieces of 2x4s cut to identical lengths for the legs. 2 pieces of 2x4s for table support. They will connect two sets of legs.
13. Poly threaded female fitting to attach to pump.
14. Intermittent timer

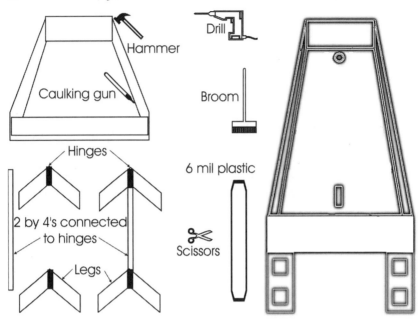

Figure 4.1: Flood table materials and tools.   *Figure 4.2: Assembled flood table.*

Tools

1. Drill.
2. 1-inch holesaw.
3. Saw.
4. Pipe wrench or crescent wrench.
5. Knife.

Setting Up the System

A. The Table

Commercial Flood Table

A commercial flood table can be placed on top of a ¾-inch plywood sheet supported with 4 cement blocks or 2 sawhorses. (Figures 4.1 and 4.2) The 2x4s should be cut to length so that when the sawhorse legs are set up, the reservoir will be slightly lower than the table. Each pair of sawhorse brackets will be joined with another 2x4 to give the table support. One or two holes will be drilled into the flood table with a holesaw. The manufacturer should specify where. Figure 4.1 shows drill with holesaw. Figure 4.2 shows the complete assembly.

Homemade Flood Table

A homemade flood table will be made of ¾-inch plywood. Anything smaller warps easily.

For simplicity, the following instructions assume that a 4x8-foot sheet of plywood is used for the table which is the size of many commercial flood tables.

Two 8-foot lengths of 1x4 or 1x6-inch wood should be nailed to the long lengths of the plywood.

One 8-foot length of 1x4 or 1x6-inch wood that is cut in half can be used for the short sides. The small sides are nailed together from the bottom of the plywood.

Caulking should be applied along the nailed seams for extra waterproofing.

The table should be placed on something that supports it, such as two sawhorses or cement blocks. Using cement blocks is the easiest method. (Figure 4.6) A quick sawhorse can be made with cheap 2x4s and hinges that the 2x4s slide

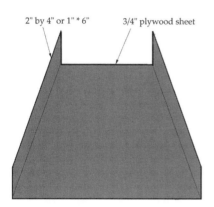

Figure 4.3: Long sides attached.

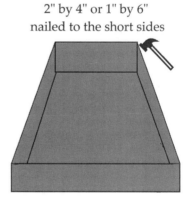

Figure 4.4: Ends attached.

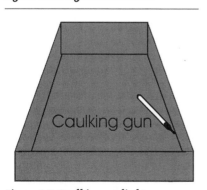

Figure 4.5: Caulking applied to seams.

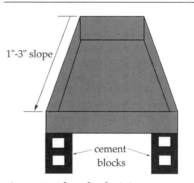

Figure 4.6: Slope for draining.

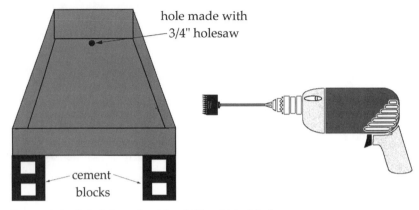

hole made with
3/4" holesaw

cement
blocks

Figure 4.7: Drain hole is made with a drill and 1-inch holesaw.

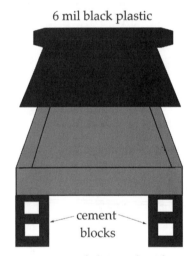

6 mil black plastic

cement
blocks

Figure 4.8: Drain hole is made with a drill and 1-inch holesaw.

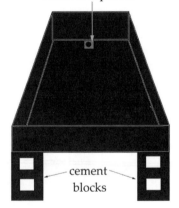

Plastic is cut away from the hole.
Wood is exposed.

cement
blocks

Figure 4.9: Exposed wood near drain hole.

into. Another 2x4 (i.e. an eight-footer for a 4x8 flood table) is placed between the hinges to complete an instant sawhorse. One end should be an inch or so higher than the other end so that the solution can be recirculated. (Figure 4.6)

In the middles of the two widths, two holes should be made about 2 inches from each end of the table using a 1-inch holesaw. Figure 4.16 shows a table with tubing connected to thru-hull fittings underneath the table.

Now, two layers of 6mm black poly plastic should be used to cover the bottom and sides of the table. It should lie nice and flat on the flood table. It can be stapled to all four sides.

A ¾-inch thru-hull fitting is inserted into the hole. Cutting plastic away from the thru-hull fitting can prevent water from trapping between the plastic layers. Cutting plastic 1 inch from the thru-hull fitting will do. (Figure 4.9)

Options:

A grower can put perlite, 70% perlite / 30% vermiculite, a Bud Blanket, or a coco mat on top of the plastic of the flood table to allow water and nutrient to be available between flood cycles. Bud blankets and Coco Mats come precut for this standard 4x8 table.

B. The pump is placed in the bottom of the reservoir and a ½-inch PVC female fitting is attached to the pump.

C. A piece of ¾-inch flex hose can be connected from the overflow pipe to the reservoir. The hose can be fed directly to the reservoir or a PVC elbow can be used. The pump can be connected to the thru-hull fitting with ½-inch tubing.

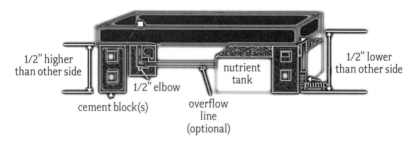

Figure 4.10: Schematic view of assembled flood table.

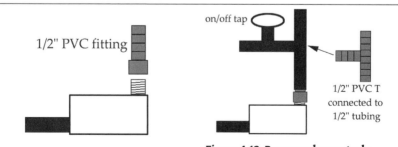

Figure 4.11: Pump attachment.

Figure 4.12: Bypass valve controls flow rate.

Heating the ½-inch tubing with hot water will make the connection easier. Figure 4.10 shows the pump and overflow pipe connected to the reservoir.

Option : Bypass valve

Just above the pump, a piece of the ½-inch tubing should be cut out and a ½-inch T should be inserted. The exposed end of the T should be connected to ½-inch tubing and then to an *on/off* tap that will act as a bypass valve.

Note:

Commercial manufacturers will have custom setups for the drain and feeding. Figures 4.13 to 4.16 show other ways that flood tables can be set up.

Feeding Methods
Rockwool or Clay

Method A: for small to larger plants

Rockwool or clay (Hydroton) in mesh pots are common mediums to use for a flood and drain system.

A grower can:

Put a 1-inch layer of perlite, 70% perlite / 30% vermiculite, a Bud Blanket, or Coco Mat on the table. This will hold air and nutrients between feedings. The

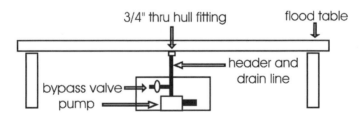

Figure 4.13 Option A: one hole in flood table.

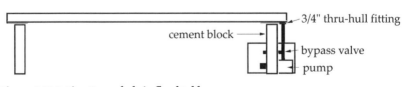

Figure 4.14 Option A: one hole in flood table.

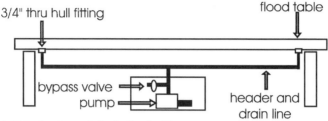

Figure 4.15 Option B: two holes in flood table.

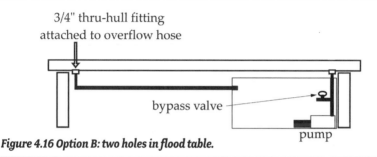

Figure 4.16 Option B: two holes in flood table.

flooding intervals can be once a day, or more often. One study done under identical growing conditions showed yields that were almost identical with one batch that was flooded continually (¼ to 1-inch flood) and the other batch that was fed in the morning.

Or:

Put a sheet of reflectix material on top of the flood table with holes cut to size to fit the containers. Reflectix will help keep the roots cooler in the day and warmer at night. The reflectix can be used without a medium on the flood table, but if there is no medium, a grower should feed a few times a day and once in the middle of darkness, if possible.

Method B: (for midsize to large plants)

A custom-sized sheet of reflectix material is precut. This material will cover the table and will fit securely over each 1-foot rockwool slab. The 1-foot rockwool slabs are placed under the holes with a secure fit. Plants can be fed 6 (or more) times during the light hours. Solution can be flooded during darkness, too.

Root bound potted plant can be sent to a flood table for quicker growth.

Soilless Mix
Method A: (for small to large plants)

1 to 4-gallon containers (mesh pots) can be placed on the table and filled with soilless mix (i.e. Sunshine #2 mix). The plants should at first be top-fed continually (for fastest growth) or periodically (slower growth with a lot less maintenance) until the roots are visible at the bottom of the container. When the roots are visible on the bottom, a grower can feed with methods A or B above.

Wick System A: Buckets

Materials

1. Two 2 to 5-gallon buckets per plant.
2. One thru-hull fitting per plant.
3. One 4-way ¾-inch fitting.
4. ¾-inch flex hose, 1 yard (meter) per plant.
5. Soilless mix, one 3.0 to 4.0 cubic foot bale.

Tools

1. Drill and 1-inch holesaw.
2. Knife.
3. Wrench.

Introduction

The wick system is a very cheap and easy hydroponic system to build. Natural cotton fibers or a lantern wick is placed ⅓ to ½ of the distance from the bottom in the top bucket that contains soilless mix. The wick must be long enough to reach the bottom of the bottom bucket to draw the solution upward with capillary action. This system does not require a pump. Figure 4.18 shows the set up and assembly of wick systems for a one plant system and figure 4.21 for a system with many plants.

Maintaining the system is simple. A master reservoir is filled with water, fertilizer is added, and the solution is delivered to the bottom container of each plant that it will feed.

There are explanations for systems with one plant or with multiple plants because the setup is slightly different.

One Plant Procedure

A. A hole is cut into the middle of the bottom of each top bucket with a 1-inch holesaw. (Figure 4.17)

B. The wick is placed into the hole so that it will be ⅓ to ½ the distance of the top bucket and long enough to contact the bottom of the lower bucket. (Figure 4.18) The wick should be of a size that will fit tightly into the hole. For example, natural cotton fibers can be twisted and tied into a 1-inch rope.

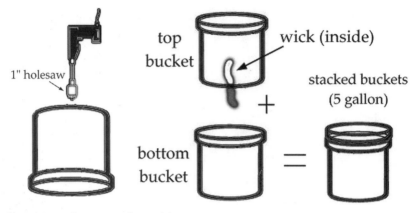

Figure 4.17 and 4.18: One plant wick setup.

C. The soilless mix is placed into the top bucket. Use your hand to hold the wick in the right place, ⅓ to ½ of the height of the bucket. The fibers can be loosened so that they spread laterally toward the sides of the bucket, but they must maintain the same height: the ⅓ to ½ rule. After the soilless mix covers the wick, let go of the wick and place more mix on top until it reaches 1 inch below the top of the bucket.

D. Top buckets with wicks are stacked into lower buckets. (Figure 4.18)

E. Mix is well moistened with water. More can be added after so that the wet soilless mix is 1 inch lower than the top.

F. The top pot is lifted out of the bottom bucket. Approximately 2 gallons of solution is added to the bottom when needed. You can use a fertilized solution for one feeding and plain water for the next. This pattern can be repeated until 2 weeks before harvest. For the last 2 weeks, the bottom wick should be cut off and the plants should be fed from the top to remove excess salts. During the flushing, the salty waste is removed from the bottom bucket.

Lighting: 1,200-watt compact fluorescent or 1,400-watt halide would be adequate lighting for one plant.

Multiple Plant Procedure
A. A hole is cut into the side of each bottom bucket and the 20-gallon reservoir.

These kind buds demonstrate complete garden care.

The hole is made 2 inches above the bottom with a 1-inch holesaw.

B. A ¾-inch thru-hull fitting is inserted into each hole and tightened with a crescent wrench. (Figure 4.21)

C. A hole is cut into the middle of the bottom of each top bucket with a 1-inch holesaw. (Figure 4.20)

D. The wick is placed into the hole so that it will be ⅓ to ½ the distance of the top bucket and long enough to contact the bottom of the lower bucket. (Figure 4.21) The wick should be of a size the will fit tightly into the hole. For example, natural cotton fibers can be twisted and tied into a 1-inch wide piece of rope.

E. The soilless mix is placed into the top buckets. A hand is used to hold the wick in the right place, ⅓ to ½ of the distance from the bottom of the bucket.

The cotton fibers can be loosened so that they spread laterally towards the sides of the bucket. But, they should maintain the same height: the ⅓ to ½ rule.

After the soilless mix covers the wick, the hand can let go of the wick and more mix is placed on top until it reaches 1 inch below the top of the bucket.

F. Top buckets with wicks are stacked into lower buckets. (Figure 4.23)

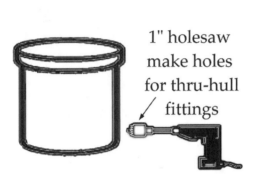

1" holesaw
make holes
for thru-hull
fittings

1" holesaw

Figure 4.19: Side hole in bottom bucket.

Figure 4.20: Center hole in plant bucket.

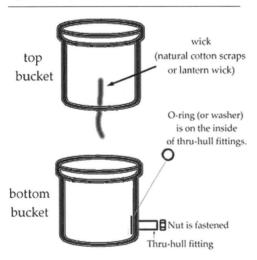

top bucket

wick
(natural cotton scraps
or lantern wick)

O-ring (or washer)
is on the inside
of thru-hull fittings.

bottom bucket

Nut is fastened

Thru-hull fitting

Figure 4.21: Inserted thru-hull fitting and wick.

cotton fibres

Figure 4.22: Wick is spread out.

Figure 4.23: Two stacked buckets.

G. Mix should be well-moistened with water. More can be added after so that the wet soilless mix is 1 inch lower than the top.

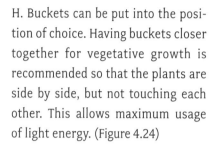

H. Buckets can be put into the position of choice. Having buckets closer together for vegetative growth is recommended so that the plants are side by side, but not touching each other. This allows maximum usage of light energy. (Figure 4.24)

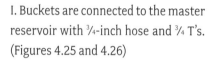

I. Buckets are connected to the master reservoir with ¾-inch hose and ¾ T's. (Figures 4.25 and 4.26)

J. As plants grow, more tubing can be connected with ¾-inch extensions to space the plants apart. (Figure 4.27) Or plants can be transplanted into an identical flowering system, except with further spacing. (Figure 4.28)

20 gallon reservoir
(i.e 20 gallon garbage can)

Figure 4.24: All buckets in position.

Growers that grow continually will use one system for vegetative growth and one for flowering.

Feeding

Maintaining the system is simple. A master reservoir is filled with water, fertilizer is added, and the solution is delivered to the bottom container of each plant it will feed.

When the solution at the bottom of the master reservoir is almost dry, more solution is added. You can use a fertilized solution for one feeding and plain water for the next. This pattern can be repeated until two weeks before harvest.

For the last two weeks, the bottom wick should be cut off and the plants

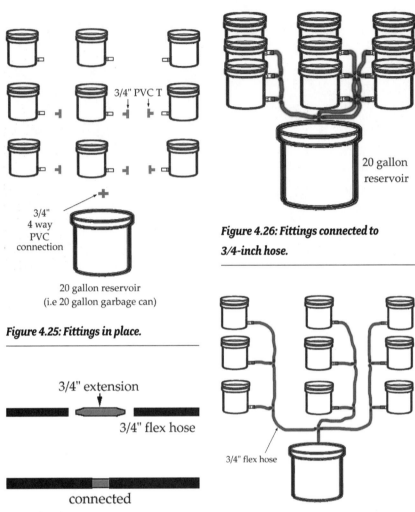

3/4" PVC T

3/4"
4 way
PVC
connection

20 gallon reservoir
(i.e 20 gallon garbage can)

Figure 4.25: Fittings in place.

Figure 4.26: Fittings connected to 3/4-inch hose.

20 gallon
reservoir

3/4" extension

3/4" flex hose

connected

3/4" flex hose

Figure 4.27 a and b: Hose extension.

Figure 4.28: Wide spacing for big plants.

should be fed from the top to remove excess salts. During the flushing, a shop vac can be used to vacuum the wasted salty water from the master reservoir. The level of the solution will be equal in all buckets. Therefore, when the master reservoir is empty, all buckets are empty.

Wick System B: Plastic Tubs

Materials

1. Plastic tub (refer to figures 4.32 for specific systems for a given space).

Crowded plants should be spaced to avoid overlapping leaves.

2. Six wicks; natural cotton fiber or lantern wicks.

3. Twenty quarts (liters) soilless mix.

Tools

1. Drill and 3½-inch holesaw or sharp knife.

2. Exacto knife or sharp knife.

3. Crescent wrench.

Introduction

This wick system is very easy to build and use. In fact, a grower can get a crop as long as there is water on the bottom of each tub. This system is used to grow a few small plants to get a series of top buds. Many salespeople in the marketplace try to dazzle buyers with reinventions, but this prehistoric growing method still has a place because small plants do not need the latest and greatest lighting, especially if the strain grows well under fluorescent lights. And these lights do not have too much heat at the source, but rather spread the heat out over a long distance. This is a fine method to grow for personal use, especially with the best light tubes available on the market. There is no work, no suspicion, and no gadgets.

Maintaining the system is simple. Water, or water and fertilizer can be added to

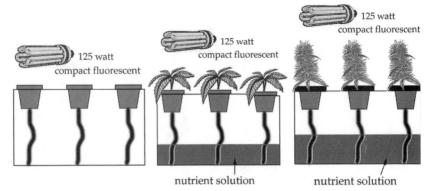

Figure 4.29, 4.30, 4.31: Garden from start to finish: pots are set-up, vegetative growth, and harvest.

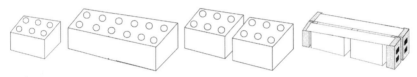

Figure 4.32: Prepared tubs for two standard 4-foot fluorescent light fixtures.

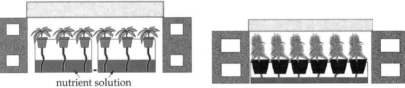

Figure 4.33: The grow medium draws nutrients.

Figure 4.34: Water is drawn into pots.

the tub. The options will be fully illustrated in this section. Soilless mix is used in each pot because it is very user-friendly and it saturates perfectly with the wick system.

Procedure

A. Holes are cut into the plastic tubs at 8-inch centers. Many plastic tubs will accommodate 5 to 6 sites; a 4-foot tub can support 10 to 12 sites. 5 to 6 plants is the perfect number for each 4-foot fluorescent fixture. (Figure 4.32) One tub will work fine with one 125-watt compact fluorescent light. (Figure 4.29)

Two tubs placed side-by-side, or one long tub 4 feet long will work well with two 4-foot fluorescent light fixtures. (Figure 4.32)

B. One foot wicks can be drawn through one of the holes in the bottom of each pot until each wick is ⅓ to ½ an inch from the bottom of each pot. The wick must reach the bottom of the tub. Natural cotton fibers or strings twisted and tied into a small rope ½ to 1-inch thick works well.

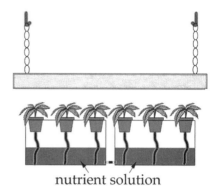

nutrient solution

Figure 4.35: Lights hung on chains.

C. Soilless mix is put into each container until it is about 1 inch from the top.

D. The soilless mix can be soaked until it is saturated. At this point, more soilless mix can be added and soaked until the mix is again 1 inch from the top of the pot.

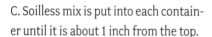
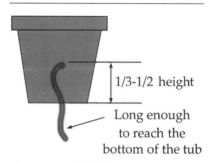

1/3-1/2 height

Long enough to reach the bottom of the tub

Figure 4.36: Wick distance.

E. Plants can be transplanted into each pot. A grower should use 4 to 5-week-old seedlings or newly rooted clones.

F. Plants can be kept 1 to 3 inches from the lights.

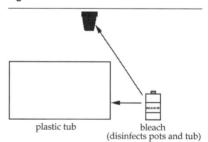

plastic tub   bleach
                (disinfects pots and tub)

G. A grower can use fertilizer at ½ strength. A liquid organic or chemical fertilizer can be used; such as Plant

Figure 4.37: Cleanliness prevents problems.

Prod 20-20-20, General Hydroponics, Greenfire Earth Juice / Bloom, Peter's 20-20-20, Supernatural BC, Dyna Bloom, or Alaska Fish Fertilizer / Alaska Bloom.

One quart (liter) of fertilized solution per plant can be put in the bottom of the tub. For example, 6 quarts for 6 plants, 12 quarts for 12 plants. The bottom of the tub can be refilled when it dries up.

H. Two weeks before harvest, the wick can be cut from each pot and the plants can be flushed from the top to remove fertilizer salts in the mix. This will upgrade the quality. A few gallons per plant should do.

I. The tubs and all pots can be reused, but they should be given a good scrub with a 10% bleach solution in water, then rinsed well of all residues with plain water. The soilless mix should be new for each crop to be on the safe side so that there are no potential disease problems.

Building Top-Feeding Systems

Option A: Flood Table
Introduction
This system is not a typical version of a commercial hydroponic system, but it can be put together with simple materials that can be found in any hardware store. If a grower happens to be in a remote location with no way out and wants a system to grow big plants quickly, this system is a valid, guaranteed option.

This system is very cheap to make and has less fittings than other top-feeding systems for big plants. Also, if a line accidentally comes out of a container, the solution will leak on the table rather than all over the floor.

Materials
1. Flood table made to size or plastic store-bought model.
2. Two ½-inch poly elbows.
3. Two ½-inch poly Ts.
4. One roll of ½-inch poly tubing.
5. Two ¾-inch thru-hull fittings.
6. One reservoir (should hold about 12 gallons of fertilized solution per each 4x4-foot table space).
7. 6ml black plastic.
8. Pump. (250 to 350 mag drive for 4x4 to 12x12-foot space. Stronger pumps can be used for larger tables.)
9. Panty hose to cover pump (optional).
10. Table support (4 cement blocks or 2 sawhorses).

Heavy duty commercial flood table.

11. Four sawhorse hinges per table.

12. ½-inch poly threaded female fitting to attach to pump.

13. Intermittent timer.

Tools

1. Drill.

2. One-inch holesaw.

3. Saw.

4. Pipe wrench or crescent wrench.

5. Knife.

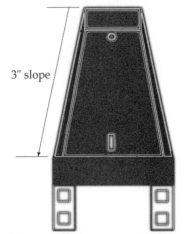

Figure 4.38: Table on cement blocks.

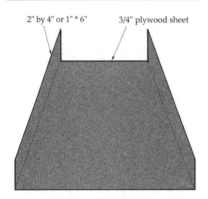

2" by 4" or 1" * 6"   3/4" plywood sheet

Figure 4.39: Long sides are connected.

2" by 4" or 1" by 6"
nailed to the short sides

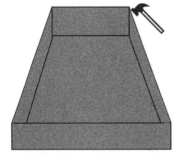

Figure 4.40: Shorts sides are nailed to plywood.

Setting Up the System

A. The Table

Commercial Flood Table

A commercial flood table can be placed on top of a ¾-inch plywood sheet supported with 4 cement blocks or 2 sawhorses. (Figure 4.38) Using cement blocks is the fastest, easiest, and cheapest method.

For a sawhorse, 2x4s should be cut to a length such that when the sawhorse legs are set up, the reservoir will be slightly lower than the table. Each pair of sawhorse brackets will be joined with another 2x4 to give the table support. One or two holes will be drilled into the flood table with a 1-inch holesaw. The manufacturer will specify where the holes are made. Figure 4.38 shows a typical setup.

Homemade Flood Table

A homemade flood table will be made of ¾-inch plywood. Anything smaller warps easily.

For simplicity, the following in-structions assume that a 4x8 sheet of plywood is used for the table, which is the size of many commercial flood tables.

Two 8-foot lengths of 1x4 or 1x6 wood should be nailed to the long lengths of the plywood. (Figure 4.39)

One 8-foot length of 1x4 or 1x6 wood that is cut in half can be used for the short sides. The small sides are

Figure 4.41: Caulking assures no leaks.

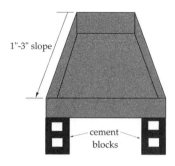

Figure 4.42: Drainage slope is critical.

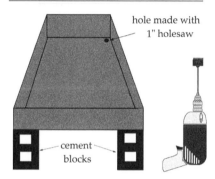

Figure 4.43: Drain hole in lowest corner.

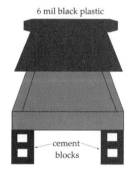

Figure 4.44: Black plastic covers the table.

nailed together from the bottom of the plywood. (Figure 4.40)

Caulking should be applied along the nailed seems for extra waterproofing. (Figure 4.41)

The table should be placed on something that supports it, such as two sawhorses or cement blocks. Using cement blocks is the easiest method. A quick sawhorse can be made with cheap 2x4 wood with hinges that the 2x4 wood slides into. Another 2x4 (i.e. an eight-footer for an 8x4 flood table) is placed between the hinges to complete an instant sawhorse. One end should be an inch or so higher than the other end so that the solution can be recirculated. (Figure 4.42)

At the lowest corner a hole is made 2 inches from the end of the table using a 1-inch holesaw. (Figure 4.43)

Now two layers of 6ml black poly plastic should be used to cover the bottom and sides of the table. (Figure 4.44) It should lie nice and flat on the flood table. It can be stapled to all four sides.

Plastic is cut away from the hole.
Wood is exposed.

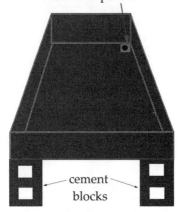

Figure 4.45: Preventing trapped water.

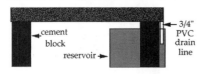

Figure 4.46: Reservoir under drain line.

1/2" PVC fitting

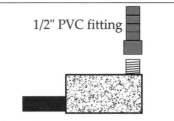

Figure 4.47: Pump connection for ½-inch hose.

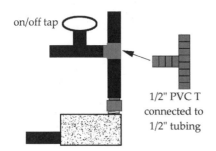

Figure 4.48: Inserted bypass valve.

A 2-foot piece of ¾-inch PVC pipe is inserted into the hole. (Figure 4.46) Cutting plastic away from the PVC pipe will prevent any water being trapped under the 6ml black plastic. (Figure 4.45)

A reservoir is placed under the drainpipe. (Figure 4.46)

B. The pump is placed in the bottom of the reservoir and a ½-inch PVC female threaded fitting is attached to the pump. (Figure 4.47)

Option: Bypass valve
Just above the pump, a piece of the ½-inch tubing should be cut out and a ½-inch T should be inserted. The exposed end of the T should be connected to ½-inch tubing and then to an *on /off* tap that will act as a bypass valve.

C. A ½-inch line is connected from the pump or the bypass valve. The hose should reach the top of the flood table. (Figure 4.48)

D. A ½-inch PVC elbow is inserted into the end of the hose.

E. A mesh pot can be stacked on an upside down mesh pot: 3 to 5-gallon mesh pots are good sizes for this system. Duct tape can be used to connect them together. (Figure 4.50) Any hydroponic medium can be used to grow the plants, such as clay, perlite, soilless mix, perlite/coconut fibers, or perlite / vermiculite. Six plants per flood table is a safe number to use to cover all square footage on the table. A small piece of tubing or a popsicle stick can be placed under the front of each bottom bucket to guarantee that the solution will drain from the bucket. (Figures 4.50)

F. ½-inch hose is run along each flood table near all of the pots. (Figure 4.52)

G. The line is cut after it reaches the last pot and a ½-inch PVC end cap is inserted. (Figure 4.52)

H. Small holes should be inserted into the ½-inch tubing that is on the flood table. A hole punch or ¹⁄₁₆-inch drill bit can be used to make the holes for the fittings. (Figure 4.51)

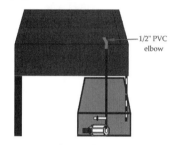

Figure 4.49: ½-inch PVC elbow is inserted.

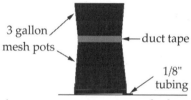

Figure 4.50: Duct tape connects buckets.

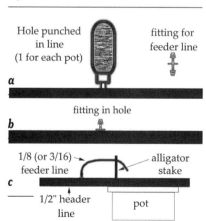

Figure 4.51 a, b, and c: Inserting a feeder line.

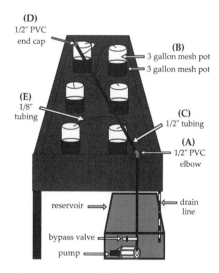

Figure 4.52: View of complete system.

View from below the plants.

I. ⅛ or ³⁄₁₆-inch tubing is connected to the fittings and each line is attached to each pot using alligator stakes. Each line should have a foot of slack because plant spacing will change as they grow larger. (Figures 4.51 and 4.52)

Feeding

If the pump runs full time the plants will grow well, especially if the water temp is near 70°F. Pumps do not use much electricity and it would be cheaper to run it full time than to buy a timer. However, the pump can be timed to run with the light cycle. There will be enough moisture left on the table to keep the bottom roots moist during the light hours. This method may be better, especially in an unattended garden where a fluke leak at night could lead to a disastrous situation if the pump was on.

But plants can be fed continuously (all day and all night), or plants can be fed intermittently. The timer can turn on and run the water for 2 minutes every 20 minutes during the light hours, or perpetually.

Cannabis has a tremendous ability to adjust to its feeding schedule. The plants will intake similar levels of water whether the pump runs intermittently or full time.

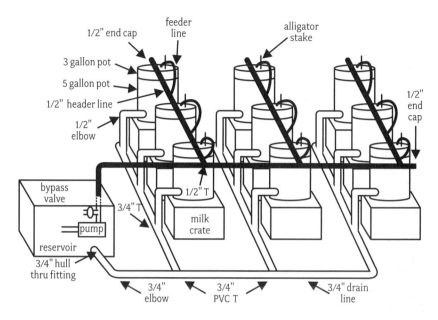

Figure 4.53: Assembled bucket system.

Option B: The Bucket System

Materials

1. One 3 to 5-gallon bucket per plant.
2. One 5-gallon bucket per plant.
3. Two ¾-inch hull-thru fittings per plant.
4. One ¾-inch T per plant.
5. ¾-inch yellow flex hose.
6. One reservoir with ¾-inch hull-thru fitting in the bottom.
7. One ¾-inch T.
8. One roll of ½-inch black poly tubing.
9. One roll of ⅛ or ³⁄₁₆-inch black poly tubing.
10. One fitting per plant to connect ½-inch tubing to ⅛ or ³⁄₁₆-inch tubing.
11. One alligator stake per plant.
12. One ½-inch T fitting.
13. One ½-inch end cap.
14. One to two ½-inch elbows.
15. One ½-inch female threaded fitting for pump.
16. One pump.

Tools
1. Drill.
2. 1-inch holesaw.
3. Knife.
4. Wrench.

Introduction:
The main use of a bucket system is to grow big plants very quickly. This system can be used for vegetative growth and flowering, but flowering is the more popular choice.

The system is used for flowering if a grower uses one room for vegetative growth and the other for flowering. Clones or 4 to 5-week-old seedlings need

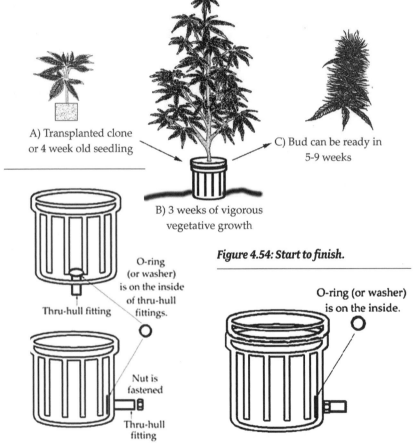

A) Transplanted clone or 4 week old seedling

C) Bud can be ready in 5-9 weeks

B) 3 weeks of vigorous vegetative growth

Figure 4.54: Start to finish.

Thru-hull fitting

O-ring (or washer) is on the inside of thru-hull fittings.

Nut is fastened

Thru-hull fitting

Figure 4.55: Inserting a thru-hull fitting.

O-ring (or washer) is on the inside.

Figure 4.56: Connected thru-hull fitting.

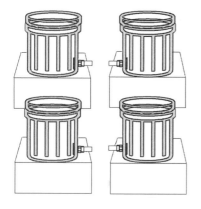

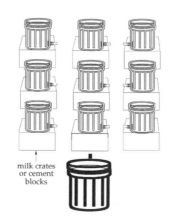

Figure 4.57: Four bucket garden.

Figure 4.58: Nine bucket setup.

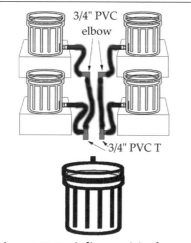

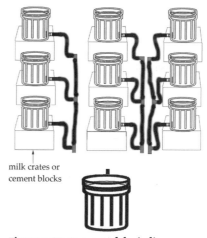

Figure 4.59: Drain lines are joined.

Figure 4.60: Connected drain lines.

about 3 weeks of vegetative growth in this system or a flood and drain system before they are induced to flower. Plants in a flood and drain system are easy to transplant into the 3-gallon pots.

Any medium can be used with this system. Using clay pellets (Hydroton) is the popular choice. Plants started in any other medium can be transplanted into this system prior to flowering.

Building the System

A bucket system can be used in a closet or a larger space. One or two plants should be plenty for a closet since plants have the potential to reach the ceiling and cover

3/4" PVC T

Figure 4.61 a and b: Reservoir is connected.

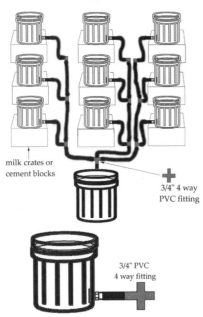

milk crates or cement blocks

3/4" 4 way PVC fitting

3/4" PVC 4 way fitting

Figure 4.62 a and b: Reservoir is attached.

the width, as long as the space for them to grow is adequate.

Plants grown in a bucket system will need about 2 to 3 weeks for vegetative growth using an 18-hour on / 6-hour off light cycle. Then they can be induced to flower with a continuous 12-hour on / 12-hour off light cycle.

With a bucket system, a 3 to 5-gallon bucket is stacked into a 5 to 7-gallon pail.

A. If a bucket is used, a ¾-inch thru-hull fitting should be inserted into the bottom so that solution can drain into the bottom pail.

B. The bottom pail should have a ¾-inch thru-hull fitting inserted in the side near the bottom. If this hole is too low, the thru-hull fitting won't fit.

C. Buckets should be placed in position. Each plant in this system can cover up to 10 square feet. Common uses for this system are 4 plants or 9 plants. 4 plants will use one 400 to 1,000-watt light, 9 plants can use four 400 to 1,000-watt lights. Therefore, they can be lined up in 2 rows of 2, or 3 rows of 3. Buckets are placed on top of milk crates or cement blocks. (Figures 4.57 and 4.58)

D. A ¾-inch elbow should be inserted into the 6-inch piece of hose of each bucket that is at the back of each row.

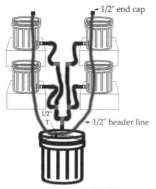

Figure 4.63: Setting up header lines.

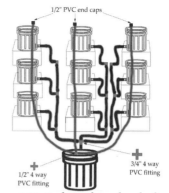

Figure 4.64: Each row has a header line.

¾-inch PVC Ts are inserted into the other ends of the 6-inch piece of hose.

The open ends of the PVC Ts and elbows should be connected to other buckets with ¾-inch flex hose. (Figures 4.59 and 4.60)

E. After all buckets are connected, there will be open ends from the ¾-inch T-fittings attached to two of the buckets. The next step is to attach these fittings to hose, then to attach them to a ½-inch PVC T or ¼ four-way PVC fitting. (Figures 4.61 and 4.62)

F. The hose is connected to the ¾-inch hull-thru fitting on the bottom of the reservoir. (Figures 4.61 and 4.62). The reservoir is located lower than the pails so the pails drain well.

G. Pieces of ½-inch poly tubing (header line) are cut and laid near the plants. (Figure 4.63 and 4.64)

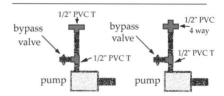

Figure 4.65: Flow rate control.

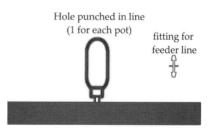

Figure 4.66: Hole for barbed fitting.

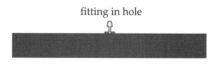

Figure 4.67: Barbed fitting tubing.

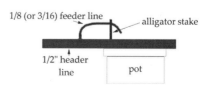

Figure 4.68: Placing the feeder line.

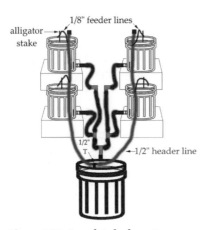

Figure 4.69: Complete hydro setup.

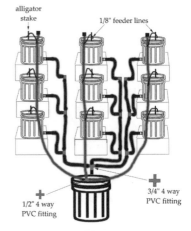

Figure 4.70: Assembled nine plant system.

H. ½-inch end caps are inserted at the end away from the reservoir. Soaking tubing in hot water allows for easier connections.

I. ½-inch black poly tubing should be connected to the ½-inch PVC T or 4-way fitting and the pump.

A recommended option is to put a bypass valve just above the pump so that the solution stays aerated and agitated, and the flow can be controlled. More ½-inch fittings can be placed on the bypass valve so that the aerated liquid is forced to the bottom near the pump. Forcing water downward can reduce any possibilities of splashing and making a mess on the floor. (Figure 4.65)

J. Small holes should be poked into the ½-inch poly header line. A punch or small drill bit can be used to make the holes for the fittings.

K. ⅛ or ³⁄₁₆-inch tubing is connected to the fittings and secured to each pot using alligator stakes. The plants can be transplanted into the buckets with the medium of choice at this time. Clay pellets (Hydroton) is the popular medium for this system

Lighting Strategies
Midsize Plants (Vegetative Growth)
Lights can be placed above the plants during vegetative growth.

Figure 4.71: *Light for small garden.*

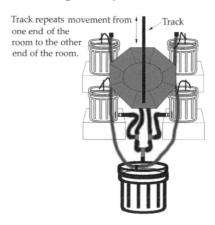

Track repeats movement from one end of the room to the other end of the room.

Track

Figure 4.72: *Light on a track.*

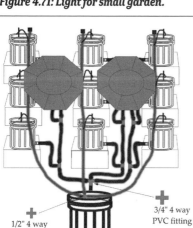

3/4" 4 way PVC fitting

1/2" 4 way PVC fitting

Figure 4.73: *Two lights for vegetative growth.*

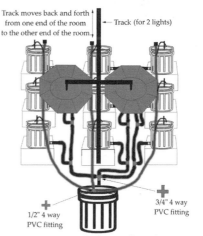

Track moves back and forth from one end of the room to the other end of the room.

Track (for 2 lights)

3/4" 4 way PVC fitting

1/2" 4 way PVC fitting

Figure 4.74: *Two lights and track.*

Large Plants (Flowering)

During flowering, lights without hoods can be placed in between the plants to give plenty of light.

For a 4 plant system, one 400, 600, or 1,000-watt bulbs could be used. Stronger bulbs can give a greater yield. Plants can be rotated frequently to illuminate them all evenly.

For a 9 plant system, four 400, 600, or 1,000-watt bulbs could be used.

Feeding

It is easiest to feed the plants with the pump running full-time during the light hours. But, plants can be fed continuously (all day and all night). Also, plants can be fed intermittently, like 2 minutes every 20 minutes during the light hours, or perpetually. An hourly timer is a cheap gadget to run the pump on a schedule such as on for 2 minutes, off for 20 minutes.

Aeroponic Conversion

A. A lid is placed on an empty top bucket.

B. A hole is made in the lid with a jigsaw or holesaw for a 3½ to 6-inch mesh pot. The mesh pot should fit snugly.

C. The feeder line is drawn through the middle of the bottom the mesh pot until it is about ½-inch below it. (Figure 4.78 and 4.79)

D. A mister is placed into the end of the feeder line. Misters come in all sizes for every tubing size. 11 to 13 Pounds per square inch (PSI) mister allows a mist at low PSI. Some misters produce a mist from 60 to 250 PSI.

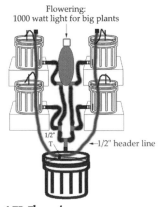

Figure 4.75: Flowering; one hoodless light.

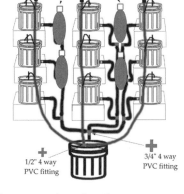

Figure 4.76: Flowering; four stationary lights.

Figure 4.77: New lid and pot.

Figure 4.78: Mesh pot.

Figure 4.79: Aero conversion completed.

Undersides of leaves should be checked regularly for bugs.

E. The pump must be able to supply a mist. A 1,200-gallon per hour pump will work for a small number or large number of pots with 11 to 13 PSI misters.

Note:
If there are leaks in the system, silicon sealant can be used to repair them after the tubing is dry. Using new ½-inch tubing and threaded fittings with teflon tape can eliminate leaks, too.

Option C: PVC Pipe System
Materials
1. One small mesh per plant (i.e. 3½-inch).
2. Two sawhorses or 4 cement blocks.
3. One alligator stake per plant.
4. One ⅛-inch fitting per plant.
5. One 8 to 12-inch piece of ⅛-inch tubing per plant.

6. One reservoir.

7. Two 4-inch elbow fittings.

8. Two 4-inch pipes cut to equal lengths that are used to hold the plants.

9. One T-fitting for each length of 4-inch pipe.

10. Mag drive pump.

11. Bypass valve.

12. ½-inch black poly tubing for header lines.

13. Two ½-inch black poly elbows.

14. ½-inch black poly Ts for each pipe.

15. ½-inch black poly end cap for each header line.

Tools

1. Drill.

2. 3½-inch holesaw.

3. Knife.

4. Wrench.

5. Handsaw or skillsaw.

Figure 4.80: Pipes on 2x4s and blocks.

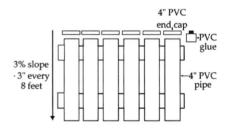

Figure 4.82: End caps joined with glue.

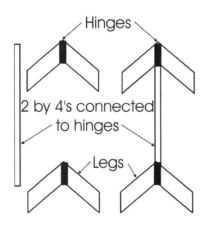

Figure 4.81: Sawhorse support option.

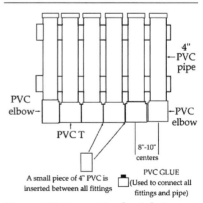

Figure 4.83: Connecting frontal pipes.

Procedure

A. The 4 to 6-inch pipe will be placed on something that supports it, like two 2x4s and four cement blocks. (Figure 4.80) A quick sawhorse can be made with cheap 2 to 3-foot lengths of 2x4 wood with hinges that the 2x4 wood slides into. Another 2x4 is placed between the hinges to complete an instant sawhorse. (Figure 4.81)

B. Two (or more) sawhorses can be used to support the connected pipes. Two sawhorses support an 8 to 12-foot length of 2x4. When the sawhorses are made, the side furthest from the reservoir should be the highest and at equal height. The side nearest the reservoir should be 1 to 3 inches lower for every 8-foot length so that the solution drains back into the reservoir.

C. All piping (i.e. 4-inch PVC) should be cut to the desired length.

D. All lengths of large pipe must have end caps attached to the higher ends that are located at the far side from the reservoir. (Figure 4.82)

E. All large 4-inch pipes except the first and last pipe are connected to their neighboring pipe with T-fittings. The first and last pipe are connected with 4-inch elbows. For example, 4-inch pipe

1" holesaw makes a hole in pipe or PVC elbow for draining solution

Drill

Figure 4.84: Making a drain hole.

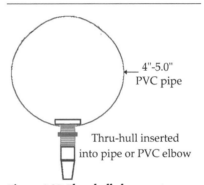

4"-5.0" PVC pipe

Thru-hull inserted into pipe or PVC elbow

Figure 4.85: Thru-hull placement.

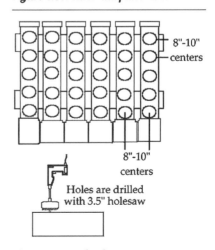

8"-10" centers

8"-10" centers

Holes are drilled with 3.5" holesaw

Figure 4.86: Holes for pots.

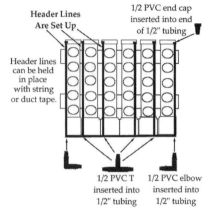

Figure 4.87: Connecting header line.

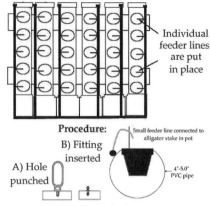

Figure 4.88: Attaching feeder lines.

will use 4-inch T-fittings. Small pieces of 4-inch pipe are placed between the T-fittings in order to connect the T-fittings and give the desired spacing (i.e. 10-inch centers). Piping and fittings can be glued with PVC cement (for PVC pipe), but the connections will be permanent. The system will not leak without glue if quality PVC is used. A little bit of duct tape can be used for securing connections so that disassembly is easy. (Figure 4.83)

Note: One of the 4-inch PVC elbows will have a ¾-inch thru-hull inserted into the bottom for draining. (Figures 4.83 and 4.84)

F. 3½-inch holes should be cut in the pipe at the desired spacing (8 to 12-inch centers). The hole sizes must match the pot sizes to make a custom fit. (Figure 4.86)

G. Header Line Setup
½-inch poly tubing should be run along the outside of the pipes until it reaches the end. It should be cut to a length that reaches the middle of the T-fittings and elbow fitting that will be connected to the larger pipe at the shorter end. The ½-inch poly tubing must have a ½-inch end cap at the end.

Another ½-inch poly line will run over the 4-inch T-fittings and the 4-inch elbows. This tubing will be connected to the other ½-inch lengths with ½-inch PVC elbows at each end and ½-inch PVC Ts for each other length of ½-inch tubing. (Figure 4.87)

H. Small holes should be punched into the ½-inch header line for the feeder tubing (i.e. ⅛, ³⁄₁₆, ¼-inch tubing) to be connected.

I. Fittings (i.e. ⅛, ³⁄₁₆, ¼-inch) should be inserted into each hole.

J. The feeder lines are connected to the fittings. The appropriate sized tubing should be connected to the fittings in the header line. For example, ³⁄₁₆-inch tubing should be connected to a ³⁄₁₆-inch fitting. The tubing should be cut to a length that will reach the larger hole (for the pots) with slack. (Figure 4.88)

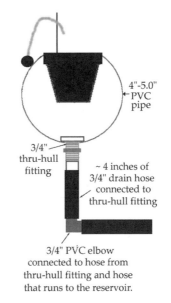

4"-5.0" PVC pipe

3/4" thru-hull fitting

~ 4 inches of 3/4" drain hose connected to thru-hull fitting

3/4" PVC elbow connected to hose from thru-hull fitting and hose that runs to the reservoir.

Figure 4.89: Drain line assembly.

K. The outside of the thru-hull fitting in the 4-inch elbow can be connected to ¾-inch hose that leads back to the reservoir.

bypass valve

pump

Figure 4.90: Bypass valve above pump.

L. A ½-inch line runs from the pump to a ½-inch PVC T that is inserted between the middle pipes. (Figure 4.91)

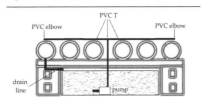

PVC elbow   PVC T   PVC elbow

drain line

pump

Recommended Option: A ½-inch poly T should be inserted a few inches above the pump that sits at the bottom of the reser-

Figure 4.91: Front view.

voir. A small 3-inch piece of ½-inch poly tubing is connected to the ½-inch T. A bypass valve should be connected to the small piece of ½-inch tubing to control the flow rate.

Feeding

It is easiest to feed the plants with the pump timer running full-time during the light hours, but plants can be fed continuously all day and all night. Or plants can be fed intermittently for 2 minutes every 20 minutes during the light hours, or for 24 hours a day.

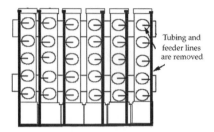

Figure 4.92: Line removal.

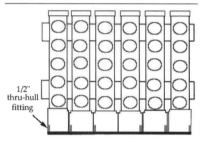

1/2"
thru-hull
fitting

Figure 4.93: New 1/2-inch lines are added.

Figure 4.94: Aero mister position.

Aeroponic Conversion

A. Each feeder line (³⁄₁₆-inch) that is connected to a pot is removed.

B. The ½-inch lines that run down the outsides of the 4-inch PVC pipes are disconnected from the ½-inch PVC Ts and elbows. (Figure 4.92)

C. Steps G to J are repeated. The slight differences are listed below.

1. A threaded fitting is used to connect the feeder tubing to the ½-inch lines.

2. The small feeder line runs through the pot. (Figure 4.94)

3. A 11 to 13-PSI mister is inserted into the end of the feeder line. (Figure 4.94)

4. The pump should be changed to a high-pressure pump designed for aeroponics. The pump should be the size required for the garden dimensions. A 1,200-gallon per hour pump will work with 11 to 13 PSI misters.

Option D: Top-Feeding V-System Using PVC Pipe

Introduction

This system uses two lights and six 4 to 5-inch PVC pipes to grow small plants. 4-inch PVC is the cheapest option.

Rooted clones or 4 to 5-week-old seedlings can be induced to flower to grow plants that will be 14 to 18 inches at maturity.

The pipes are placed in V position. This system can produce more volume per square foot than the flat PVC pipe system.

A novice grower could place a medium on the bottom of each pipe for the roots.

Materials

All materials and step-by-step construction for this system will be given on the next pages.

Tools

1. Saw.
2. Drill.
3. 3 to 3½-inch holesaw.
4. Line punch or ¹⁄₁₆-inch drill bit.
5. Exacto knife or sharp knife.
6. One-inch holesaw.
7. Hammer.
8. Crescent wrench.

Construction

The PVC pipes can be placed on a support system made with 2x4s or cement blocks. The support system is lighter. The instructions for the building of this system use the 2x4 frame, but if the construction is done with cement blocks, the setup remains the same.

Frame

A. Two 3-foot pieces of 2x4 wood are nailed together with 3 to 4-inch nails to make a 90° angle. (Figure 4.98)

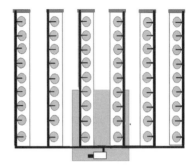

Figure 4.95: Top view of system.

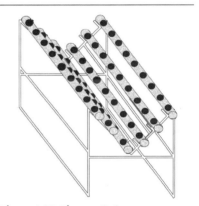

Figure 4.96: Pipes on 2x4s.

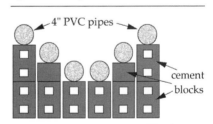

Figure 4.97: Pipes on cement blocks.

B. Both sides should be cut at a 45° angle at 2 feet high. (Figure 4.99)

C. Three 6-inch pieces of 2x4 are nailed to each side of the V-shaped piece of wood. (Figure 4.100)

D. The V is nailed to two 4-foot pieces of 2x4. (Figure 4.101)

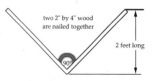

Figure 4.98: Connected V.

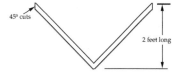

Figure 4.99: Ends are cut.

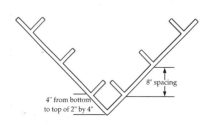

Figure 4.100: 6-inch pieces are added.

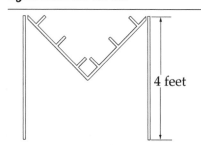

Figure 4.101: V nailed to 2x4s.

E. The M-shaped pieces are connected together with two 7 to 8-foot pieces of 2x4.

F. Two 7 to 8-foot pieces of 2x4 are nailed halfway up the lengths for additional support.

G. Two 2x4s are nailed from V to V.

H. Two pieces of 2x4 are nailed to the front and back of the frame for extra support.

I. Holes are cut into the pipes at 8 to 10-inch centers. This is 9 to 11 sites per 8-foot piece of pipe.

J. Pipes are placed on stand.

K. A 1-inch holesaw is used to cut holes on the bottom of each pipe for thru-hull fittings. The hole is made in the front.

L. A reservoir goes under the system. (Figure 4.111)

M. A ¾-inch thru-hull fitting is inserted into each pipe.

N. 4-inch PVC end caps are connected to both ends of the PVC pipe. PVC glue is used to fasten the end caps.

Healthy seeds ready for germination.

The shell popping through the soil is the first sign of germination.

These round leaves will fall off; the pointed ones are the first 'true' leaves.

These 'true' leaves will grow in the opposite direction from the first leaves.

This healthy clone is growing rapidly.

Plants that receive less lighting have larger spaces between the plant nodes, flower a little later, and produce less bud.

Some seedlings can develop strange growths while others will be completely healthy under the same conditions.

Tops that receive too much light or heat, or too little nutrients, can turn yellow.

Small buds in the plant nodes can be used for plant rejuvenation and breeding purposes.

Green leaves from top to bottom indicate desirable growth.

Small immature buds in the nodes can be removed for quick samples of the stock.

A nice harvest is coming!

Track lights provide equal distribution.

Horizontal hoods light up this garden.

This 2x4 wood shelving supports a smell removal unit and lights.

Tiers of fluorescent lights allow hundreds of clones to be rooted in a small amount of space.

Cheap 2x2s are nailed together to make a custom garden set-up.

Many unopened male pollen sacks.

Pollen is released from the opened sacks.

Yellowing, purple leaves indicate that plants have been successfully flushed.

Vegetative growth in 2-gallon pots.

This efficient garden has maximized the ratio of floor space to growing space.

Shoot is cut with exacto knife.

Shoot is removed from plant in vegetative growth.

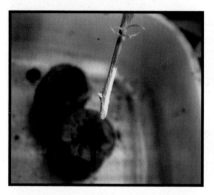

Nodes are dipped in a powder rooting hormone.

Clones are placed in expanded jiffy cubes.

First visible roots come out of the bottom.

Clone is ready to transplant to any medium.

Top feeding hydroponic system delivers nutrients to plants growing in rockwool cubes.

Budding plants in 2-gallon pots.

Mold can hit small sections of bud without spreading elsewhere.

Powdery mildew may not stop plants from producing, but it can easily cover all plants in a humid room.

Improper feeding and contaminated growing mediums can stunt plants. Some mediums can be safely reused, but, disposable mediums like rockwool cannot.

Brown mold should be completely cut out of all buds as soon as it is detected in order to stop it from spreading.

Leaves can show tell tale signs like deficiencies, disease, and pest damage.

Early colas show that rewards are blooming.

String: a useful item for plant training.

Ganga growing towards the vertically stacked lights in the middle.

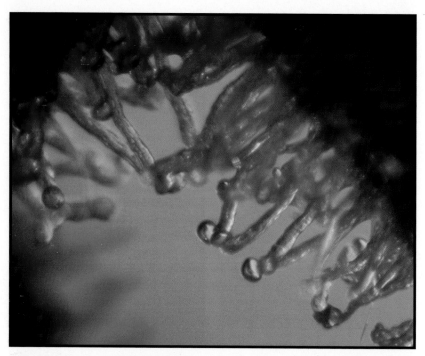

Resin glands protruding from the bud.

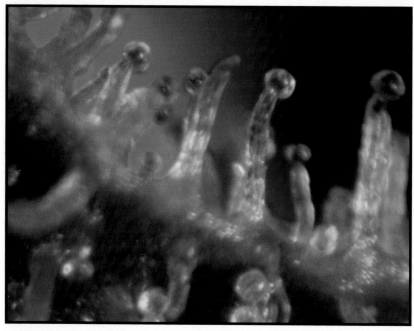

Macro shot of resin glands.

Marijuana in late flower.

After months of care, she is near the end of her life cycle.

Leafy buds are tedious to pick.

This bud has been expertly trimmed.

Fan leaves make picking easier.

Super mature top.

Pots are placed side by side until, through growth, they need to be spaced out.

Large budding plants need proper care to reach their potential.

Pump sprayers make foliar feeding and pesticide use simple.

Crystals spread far down these fan leaves.

For some, the more crystal the better.

Bud clusters surround the stalk.

Brown, wrinkled hairs indicate ripeness.

Buds go into one pile and the trim goes into another.

Limbs are cut from the plant to manageable lengths for trimming.

The dried fruits of your labor.

O. The header line is set up. (Figure 4.111)

1. A piece of ½-inch tubing is connected from the pump to a ½-inch PVC T.

2. Two pieces of ½-inch tubing are connected to the ½-inch PVC T. The tubing must reach the highest pipes on each side.

3. ½-inch PVC elbows are attached to the ends of the tubing.

4. ½-inch PVC Ts are inserted into the tubing next to the other big pipes.

5. ½-inch tubing (8 feet) is connected to each ½-inch PVC elbow and ½-inch PVC T.

6. ½-inch PVC end caps are inserted into the end of all ½-inch tubing.

P. The feeder line is set up.

1. A hole is made in the ½-inch tubing next to each plant site using a hole punch.

2. A barbed fitting is inserted into each line. ⅛ to ³⁄₁₆-inch fittings work fine.

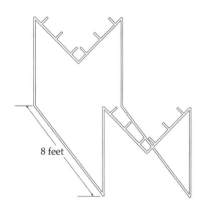

Figure 4.102: Both M shapes joined.

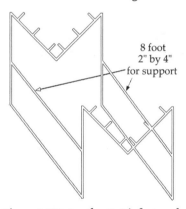

8 foot
2" by 4"
for support

Figure 4.103: Another 2x4 is fastened.

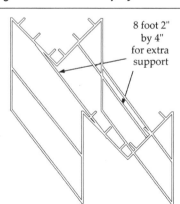

8 foot 2"
by 4"
for extra
support

Figure 4.104: More support.

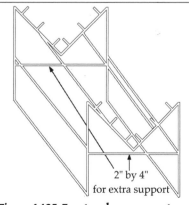

2" by 4"
for extra support

Figure 4.105: Front and rear support.

Holes are made with 3.0"-3.5" holesaw

Figure 4.106: Spaced holes are cut.

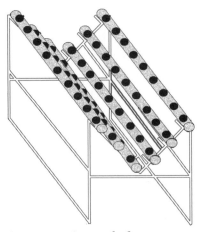

Figure 4.107: Pipes on the frame.

Figure 4.108: Drain hole for each pipe.

Figure 4.109: Thru-hull for drain line.

4" end caps

4" PVC pipe

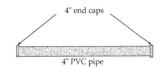

Figure 4.110: End caps for each side.

Line Punch

Barbed fitting goes into hole.

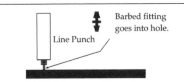

Figure 4.112: Hole punch.

1/2" PVC end caps

1/2" header line

1/2" PVC elbow

1/2" PVC T

1/2" PVC T

pump

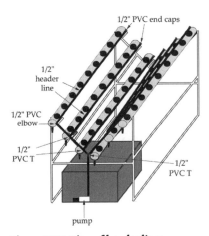

Figure 4.111: View of header lines.

alligator stake

1/8" tubing

1/2" header line

4"-5.0" PVC pipe

3/4" thru-hull fitting

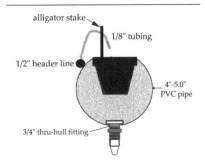

Figure 4.113: Attached feeder line.

3. One-foot of ⅛ to ³⁄₁₆-inch tubing is cut for each plant site.

4. Plants can be transplanted into a medium such as clay or lava rock. Hydroton clay pellets are a popular choice. The pots with plants can be placed securely in each hole.

5. An alligator stake should be placed into each 3 to 3½-inch mesh pot.

6. The one-foot line is drawn through the hole in the alligator stake so that the solution will pour into the pot.

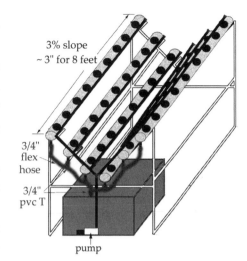

Figure 4.114: 3% slope for drainage.

7. The other end of the 1-foot piece of tubing is attached to the fitting in the ½-inch tubing.

Q. The drain line is set up. (Figure 4.114)

1. The four lowest ¾-inch thru-hull fittings are connected to ¾-inch PVC s with 6-inch pieces of ¾-inch flex hose.

2. The highest thru-hull fittings on each side are connected to the nearest ¾-inch PVC Ts with the flex hose.

3. The lowest and second-lowest thru-hull fittings are connected to one another with flex hose.

4. The lowest thru-hulls are connected together with a ¾-inch PVC T.

5. The loose end of the ¾-inch PVC T is connected to flex hose that runs inside the reservoir.

Lighting

P. Two lights can be placed ⅓ the distance from each end.

Two 1,000-watt lights would need to run off of a 240-volt circuit like a dryer or oven or a 30-amp fuse at the breaker box.

A 1,000-watt light and a 400-watt light, or two 600-watt lights could run on a regular 15-amp household circuit.

Track lighting could be used with 2 lights. (Figure 4.116)

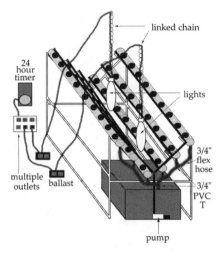

Figure 4.115: Lights and timer.

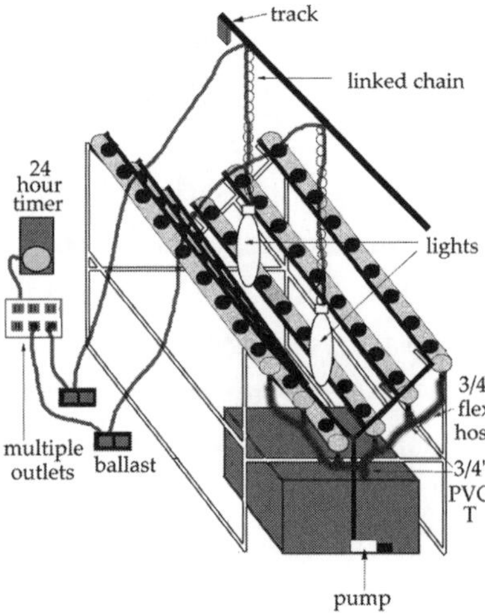

Figure 4.116: Track lighting.

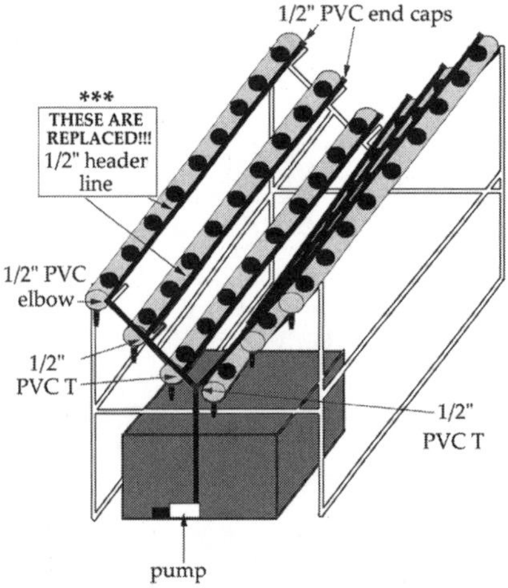

Figure 4.117: First conversion step.

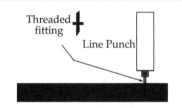

Figure 4.118: Adding a threaded fitting.

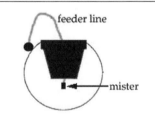

Figure 4.119: Mister in place.

Aeroponic Conversion

A. Each feeder line (³/₁₆-inch) that is connected to a pot is removed.

B. The ½-inch lines that run down the outsides of the 4-inch PVC pipes are disconnected from the ½-inch PVC Ts and elbows. (Figure 4.117)

C. New ½-inch lines replace the old ones.

The setup is identical to the top-feeding construction on page 66 except for the slight differences listed below.

Hydro bud: high quality, and fast.

1. A threaded fitting is used to connect the feeder tubing to the ½-inch lines.

2. The small feeder line runs through the pot. (Figure 4.119)

3. An 11 to 13-PSI mister is inserted into the end of the feeder line. (Figure 4.119)

4. The pump should be changed to a high-pressure pump designed for aeroponics. The pump should be the size required for the garden dimensions. A 1,200-gallon per hour pump will work with 11 to 13-PSI misters.

Column System A: Hand-Feeding System Using 2x4s and Pots

Materials

1. One 1-gallon pot per plant.

2. One 6-inch plant dish per plant.

3. Nails.

4. 2x4s: twelve 6-foot pieces for a twelve-column system; twenty-eight 6-foot pieces for a twenty-eight pipe column system.

    2x4s options: twelve columns, seventy-two 8-inch pieces; twenty-eight columns, one-hundred-sixty-eight 8-inch pieces.

5. One 3-gallon pot for each column: 12 pots for 12 columns, 28 pots for 28 columns.

6. 20-gallon garbage can.

7. Hand-watering can.

8. Contact cement.

Tools

1. Handsaw or skillsaw.

2. Hammer.

3. Exacto knife (or sharp knife.)

Introduction

In most cases, this system is used to grow small plants.

    Seedlings can be induced to flower at 5 weeks old, clones at 6.

    Typical uses for this system are 12 pipes at 8-inch centers or 10 pipes at 10-inch centers using three 400-watt lights. Or 28 pipes at 8-inch centers, or 24 pipes at 10-inch centers using two 1,000-watt lights. (Figure 4.126) This section describes a 12-pipe system.

    This system is the cheapest and easiest column system to use for the novice. It will use soilless mix inside of each 1-gallon pot.

    The feeding in this system can be done daily or weekly.

    This system is not pretty, but it will cost less than $100 to build. Considering that competitive systems can run $2,000 to buy, this may be an option worth trying for those who need the look and feel of plants in pots rather than a gardening system that looks like something that could be used on Mars.

Procedure

A. All 2x4s are cut to 6-foot lengths with a handsaw or skillsaw. This is really easy, especially if they are purchased in 12-foot lengths. (Figure 4.120)

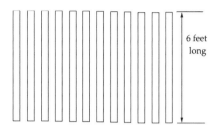

Figure 4.120: 6-foot 2x4s.

B. Starting at 8 inches from the top of each 6-foot piece of wood, the small 8-inch pieces of 2x4 or 1x6 inches are nailed into the wood at 8-inch centers with 4-inch nails until there are 6 pieces nailed into each long length. (Figure 4.121)

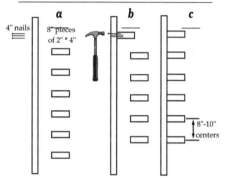

Figure 4.121 a, b and c: Fastening plant holders.

C. Holes should be made in the center of each lid to fit the long 2x4-inch. (Figure 4.122) If there are no lids the construction can continue.

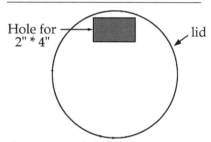

Figure 4.122: Hole in lid for 2x4.

D. The lengths can be nailed into the center or backside of the 3-gallon buckets. (Figures 4.123 and 4.124)

E. The 3-gallon buckets should be filled with sand, stones, or cement to keep the wood in the center and give the system support. If the bucket has a lid, it can be secured after bucket is filled.

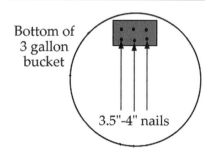

Figure 4.123: 2x4 nailed to bucket.

F. Plant dishes can be glued to the extended pieces of wood with contact cement. (Figure 4.124) Or 1x6-inch wood can be nailed to the extended

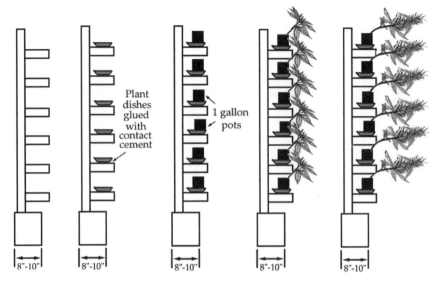

Figure 4.124: From start to finish.

pieces of 2x4-inch. If plant dishes are not used, a tarp or sheet of plastic should be placed on the floor so that the floor stays clean.

G. The 1-gallon pots can be filled with soilless mix and watered until they are soaked.

H. The plants can be transplanted into each pot and placed on top of the plant dishes; 20 to 30 plants can be placed on the floor to maximize the yield.

Lighting
I. Three 400-watt lights can be hung from the ceiling for a 10 to 12 pipe system. (Figure 4.125) Hooks for the lights should be screwed into a stud. But, if no stud is available in the desired spot, a 3 to 4-inch piece of 2x4 can be nailed to the nearest studs with 3 to 4-inch nails. The lights can be hung on any part of the 2x4. Or two 1,000-watt lights can be hung from the ceiling for a 28-pipe system.

J. The lights can placed 1-foot from each plant. The buckets can easily be moved to allow grower to increase or decrease light intensity. The buckets will be in a circle around the lights. (Figure 4.126)

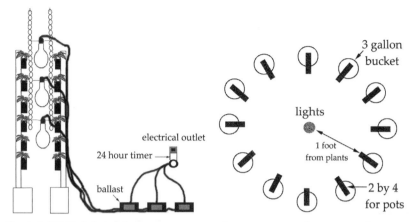

Figure 4.125: Lighting technique.   Figure 4.126: Complete system placement.

Feeding
K. The feeding can either be daily, or when needed.

Novice Tip
A grower can water with fertilizer each time the plant needs water. Since these plants are small, that could be as little as once a week. Two weeks before harvesting, plants should get no more fertilizer, just plain water. A grower should flush each plant with a few gallons of water two weeks before harvest. Afterward, only plain water is added when necessary.

A grower can shoot for 2 to 3 pounds of dried bud; ¼-ounce per plant.

Column System B: Top-Feeding / Aeroponic System Using PVC Pipe with Containers
Materials
1. One 2-inch mesh per plant, if necessary.
2. One ⅛-inch fitting per plant.
3. One piece of ⅛-inch tubing per plant that is connected from header line to container.
4. One reservoir.
5. Four-inch PVC pipe that is cut to equal lengths that are used to hold the plants.
6. Pump.
7. Bypass valve.

8. ½-inch black poly tubing for header lines.

9. ½-inch black poly elbows.

10. ½-inch black poly Ts.

11. ½-inch black poly end caps.

12. ¾-inch flex hose.

13. One 3-gallon bucket per pipe.

14. ¾-inch thru-hull fittings.

15. ¾-inch end cap.

16. 6ml black poly.

17. Twine.

18. Contact cement.

Tools

1. Drill.

2. One-inch hole saw.

3. Exacto knife.

4. Crescent wrench.

5. Custom-sized holesaw (i.e. 3½-inch) for plant containers, if necessary.

6. Handsaw or skillsaw.

Introduction

In most cases, this system is used to grow small plants. Seedlings can be induced to flower at 5 weeks old, or clones that have reached a height of 6 inches.

Typical uses for this system are 12 pipes at 8-inch centers or 10 pipes at 10-inch centers using three 400-watt lights. Or 28 pipes at 8 i nch centers, or 24 pipes at 10-inch centers using two 1,000-watt lights. But a grower can use half of the pipes described above and double the spacing to grow midsize plants.

This system is a fast, cheap, and easy column system to build. This system will use a medium like soilless mix in the pipe. Soilless mix is the easiest choice.

The feeding in this system can be done continually, or for 2 minutes every 20 minutes.

Procedure
Plant-Holding Components

A. First you'll need to choose the desired pipe. 4 to 8-inch PVC is a good pipe to

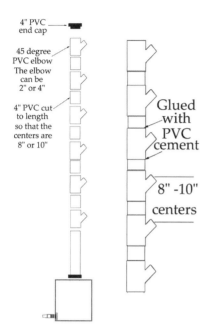

4" PVC end cap

45 degree PVC elbow The elbow can be 2" or 4"

4" PVC cut to length so that the centers are 8" or 10"

Glued with PVC cement

8" -10" centers

Figure 4.127: On the left parts unassembled, on the right assembled.

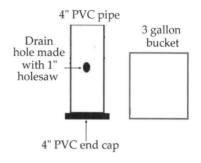

4" PVC pipe

Drain hole made with 1" holesaw

3 gallon bucket

4" PVC end cap

Figure 4.128: Drain hole option.

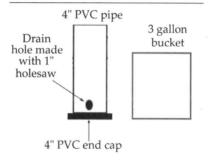

4" PVC pipe

Drain hole made with 1" holesaw

3 gallon bucket

4" PVC end cap

Figure 4.129 a: Drain hole option.

use. 4-inch is the cheapest but larger pipe is easier to use because there is more room for the roots. To keep things simple, these instructions are with 4-inch PVC.

45°, 4-inch PVC elbows are used for the plant holders. (Figure 4.127)

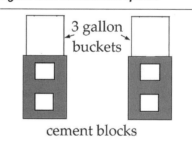

3 gallon buckets

cement blocks

Figure 4.129 b: Buckets on blocks.

B. All 4-inch piping should be cut into small, 6-inch pieces so that when they are glued with the 45° PVC elbows the distance between plants will be 8 to 10 inches center. (Figure 4.127)

The 4-inch piping is glued with PVC cement to the 4-inch PVC elbows so that the space is 8 to 10 inches center.

C. The tops of the pipes will have 4-inch PVC end caps attached loosely to the top to keep out light. The cap should be able to be removed easily. (Figure 4.127)

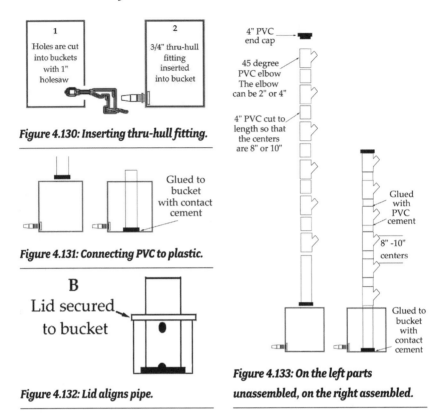

Figure 4.130: Inserting thru-hull fitting.

Figure 4.131: Connecting PVC to plastic.

Figure 4.132: Lid aligns pipe.

Figure 4.133: On the left parts unassembled, on the right assembled.

D. One piece of 4-inch PVC should be cut at a height of a few inches to a foot above the buckets. A 4-inch end cap should be glued to the bottom with PVC glue. (Figure 4.128)

E. Option 1:
A hole should be made just below the height of the 3-gallon bucket to drain the solution. (Figure 4.128) The buckets should have a diameter less than the center spacing of 8 to 10 inches.

Option 2:
Pipe is filled with medium like soilless mix. If pipe is filled with medium, the bucket should be placed on 1-foot (or higher) cement blocks to allow for drainage. The drain hole should be just above the end cap. (Figure 4.129)

Drain Components
F. Each bucket at the base of the piping should have one hole made about 2 inch-

es from the bottom on each side using a 1-inch holesaw for ¾-inch thru-hull fittings that will be inserted into each hole. (Figure 4.130)

G. The 4-inch PVC pieces (from step D) can be glued to the bottoms of each bucket with contact cement. The top of each pipe should be at least 1-foot higher than the bucket. The placement in the bucket should be dead center. (Figure 4.131)

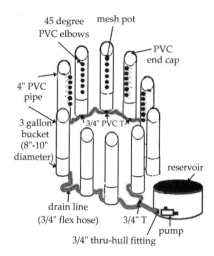

Figure 4.134: Complete drainage assembly.

H. Each bucket lid should have a hole made into it to fit around the pipe. The lid will add extra support to the pipes and make for less water loss through evaporation. The lid can be placed on the bucket when the glue is dry. Holes can be made with a 4 ¼-inch holesaw, hacksaw, or jigsaw.

I. The columns can be glued with PVC cement to the 4-inch pipe. (Figure 4.133) The columns can be on the same side or opposite side as the thru-hull fittings.

J. The pipes should be placed in a circle to be 1-foot + plant distance from bulbs in middle. (Figure 4.134)

K. 6-inches of ¾-inch drain hose is attached to each thru-hull fitting. (Figure 4.134)

L. A ¾-inch PVC T is attached to each piece of 6-inch hose. (Figure 4.134)

M. All drain buckets are connected to each other with tubing that is connected to ¾-inch thru-hull fittings. (Figure 4.134) This is like a chain that can be shaped any way that is desired in order to place plants at optimum light distances. (Figure 4.134)

N. The first bucket nearest the reservoir will connect to the ¾-inch thru-hull fitting in the reservoir. (Figure 4.134)

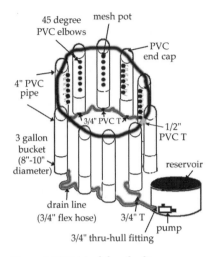

Figure 4.135: ½-inch header line.

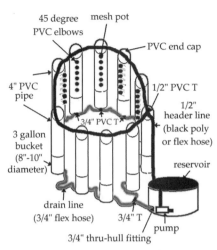

Figure 4.136: Header line attached to pump.

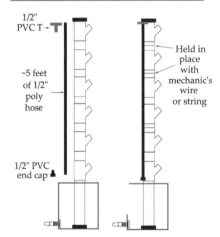

Figure 4.137: on the left header line
unassembled, on the right assembled.

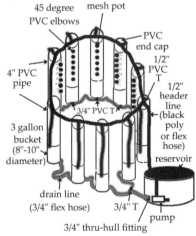

Figure 4.138: Vertical header lines.

Feeder Line Components

0. 1. A long piece of ½-inch poly tubing should run along the tops of the pipes
until it reaches the last one in the circle.

2. A ½-inch PVC T is inserted at the end. (Figure 4.135)

3. The open end of the ½-inch PVC T is connected to a line that runs to the pump
at the bottom of the reservoir. A 20-gallon reservoir will do. (Figure 4.136)

4. The main line is cut at each pipe, and a ½-inch PVC T is installed for each length

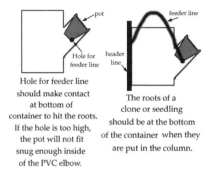

Hole for feeder line
should make contact
at bottom of
container to hit the roots.
If the hole is too high,
the pot will not fit
snug enough inside
of the PVC elbow.

The roots of a
clone or seedling
should be at the bottom
of the container when they
are put in the column.

Figure 4.139: Feeder line placement.

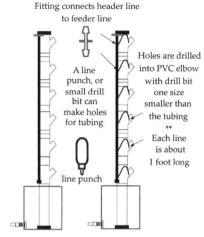

Figure 4.140 : Installing feeder ines.

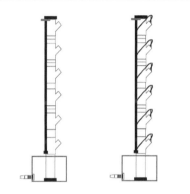

Figure 4.141: Feeder lines hooked up.

The medium should
be well draining
for top-feeding in
the column.

Clay, lava rock
and perlite
are safe choices.

Figure 4.142: Exterior feeder line.

of vertical pipe. (Figure 4.137)

5. The PVC T is connected to pieces of ½-inch poly tubing that run down the sides of the large piping to a height just above the top of the reservoir. (Figure 4.138)

6. The poly tubing is connected to ½-inch PVC end caps.

7. Holes are punched and appropriate connection fittings are inserted, such as ⅛-inch fittings for ⅛-inch lines. One fitting is used for each plant.

8. Lines are cut to a length that reaches each plant container with a little slack and inserted into the connection fittings. There are two options. (Figures 4.139 and 4.140 or 4.141 and 4.142)

9. Lines are then connected to alligator stakes.

P. The pump is connected to the ½-inch poly tubing that reaches the bottom of the reservoir. (Figure 4.143)

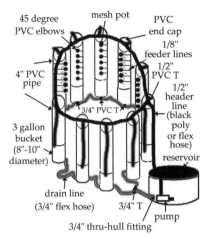

45 degree PVC elbows

mesh pot

PVC end cap

1/8" feeder lines

1/2" PVC T

4" PVC pipe

1/2" header line (black poly or flex hose)

3/4" PVC T

3 gallon bucket (8"-10" diameter)

reservoir

drain line (3/4" flex hose)

3/4" T

pump

3/4" thru-hull fitting

Figure 4.143: Complete assembly.

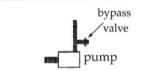

bypass valve

pump

Figure 4.144: The bypass valve.

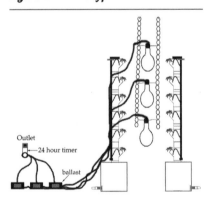

Outlet

24 hour timer

ballast

Figure 4.145: Lights and plants.

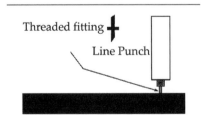

Threaded fitting

Line Punch

Figure 4.146: Threaded fitting for aero.

Option:

A bypass valve can be inserted between the pump and the first ½-inch PVC elbow.

To insert a bypass valve:

1. A 1-inch chunk is cut out of the ½-inch poly line.

2. A ½-inch PVC T is inserted into the cut out section.

3. A 5-inch chunk of ½-inch poly plastic is connected to the ½-inch PVC T.

4. A lightweight plastic tap is connected to the 5-inch chunk of 5-inch black poly piece.

Lighting

Q. Lights are hung in between the plants without hoods. For example, three or four 400-watt lights (2 to 3 sodiums and 1 halide) can be placed on top of each other to illuminate the plants grown in 6-foot high pipe.

Feeding

R. It is easiest to feed the plants with the pump timer running full-time, only during the light hours. But, plants can be fed continuously (all day and all night). Also, plants can be fed intermittently (i.e. every 20 minutes for 2 minutes, every 2 to 5 minutes for 30 seconds) during all hours.

Detailed feeding options and instructions are provided in chapter 5.

Aeroponic Conversion

Making the aeroponic version of this system is easier than making the top-feeding system.

A. The lines that run down the outsides of the column will be cut from the small feeder lines and disconnected from the ½-inch PVC Ts and removed from the ½-inch PVC T. (Figure 4.141)

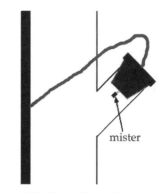

Figure 4.147: Mister through pot.

B. A new piece of identically sized ½-inch hose is cut.

C. The ½-inch end cap from the old tubing is put in one end of the new tubing.

D. The new ½-inch tubing is reconnected to the PVC T and is connected to the feeder tubing with threaded fittings. (Figure 4.146)

E. An 11 to 13 PSI mister is inserted into the end of the feeder line, then placed in position. (Figure 4.147)

F. The pump should be changed to a high-pressure pump designed for aeroponics. The pump should be the size required for the garden dimensions. A 1,200-gallon per hour pump will work with 11 to 13 PSI misters. High-pressure pumps are available at hydroponic stores, water supply places, and on the Internet.

Column System C: Top-Feeding Using 4-inch PVC Pipe

Materials

1. One reservoir for feeding.
2. One reservoir for flushing.
3. Four-inch PVC pipe; 6 feet per column.
4. Pump.
5. Bypass valve.

6. ½-inch black poly tubing for header lines.

7. ½-inch black poly elbows.

8. ½-inch black poly T's.

9. ½-inch black poly end caps.

10. ¾-inch flex hose.

11. One bucket per pipe to collect runoff solution.

12. ¾-inch thru-hull fittings.

13. ¾-inch end cap.

14. ⅛-inch tubing for feeder lines (1-foot per plant).

15. Twine.

16. PVC glue.

17. Contact cement.

Tools

1. Exacto knife.

2. Crescent wrench.

3. Scissors.

4. Drill.

Introduction

In most cases this system is used to grow small plants. Seedlings can be induced to flower at 5 weeks old, while clones can be induced to flower when they are 6 inches tall.

Typical uses for this system are to set up 12 pipes at 8-inch centers or 10 pipes at 10-inch centers using two 1,000-watt lights.

The pipes will be filled with a medium; anything from soilless mix to a homemade blend like 30% coco fibres / 70% perlite.

With this system, the pipes can be empty so that the roots run freely down the inside of the pipes, or the pipes can be filled with a medium like soilless mix. If they have mix, feeding once a day will ensure that the medium does not dry out and plants get ample nutrition. If the pipes are empty, having the pump run for 2 minutes every 20 minutes will keep the root zone moist and with a good supply of plant food.

Procedure

A. All 4-inch piping should be cut to 5 feet. (Figure 4.148)

Column systems have the best bud : time and space devoted to growing ratio.

B. An end cap is glued into the bottom of each pipe with PVC glue. (Figure 4.149)

C. A hole is made with a 1-inch holesaw just above the end cap. (Figure 4.150)

D. Holes are drilled into the 6-foot PVC pipe at 8 to 10-inch centers with a hole-saw. The holes need to be large enough for the plant and its roots. Smaller plants such as rooted clones are easier to work with.

E. A thru-hull fitting is inserted into each bucket. A 1-inch holesaw is used to make the hole. A crescent wrench is used to fasten it securely in place. (Figure 4.152)

F. The support system is now built: there are two options.

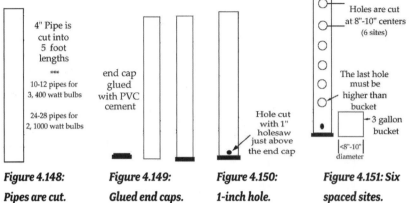

4" Pipe is cut into 5 foot lengths

***

10-12 pipes for 3, 400 watt bulbs

24-28 pipes for 2, 1000 watt bulbs

end cap glued with PVC cement

Hole cut with 1" holesaw just above the end cap

Holes are cut at 8"-10" centers (6 sites)

The last hole must be higher than bucket

3 gallon bucket

<8"-10" diameter

Figure 4.148: Pipes are cut.

Figure 4.149: Glued end caps.

Figure 4.150: 1-inch hole.

Figure 4.151: Six spaced sites.

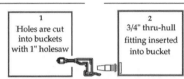

1
Holes are cut into buckets with 1" holesaw

2
3/4" thru-hull fitting inserted into bucket

Figure 4.152: Inserting a thru-hull fitting.

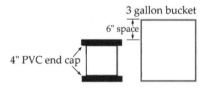

3 gallon bucket

6" space

4" PVC end cap

Figure 4.153: Gluing end caps.

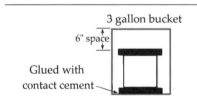

3 gallon bucket

6" space

Glued with contact cement

Figure 4.154: Joining PVC to plastic.

Option A:

1. A piece of 4-inch PVC is cut and has an end cap glued to both sides with PVC cement. The whole piece should be 6 inches lower than the bucket. (Figure 4.153)

2. This piece of pipe (with end caps) is glued to the bottom of a bucket with contact cement.

3. The end caps of the long pipe and short pipe are glued together with PVC cement. The holes in the long pipe should be aligned above the thru-hull fitting. (Figure 4.155)

3. The bucket lid is placed over the pipe and secured to the bucket.

The lids are placed over the tops of the pipes to give a tight fit. Holes can be cut into the center of the lids with a holesaw, jigsaw, or hacksaw.

4. Four-inch PVC pipes are filled up with medium (i.e. soilless mix) or they can be filled after the complete setup. Duct tape placed over the holes will prevent the mix from leaking. The mix should be nice and wet before the holes are exposed so that it does not fall out.

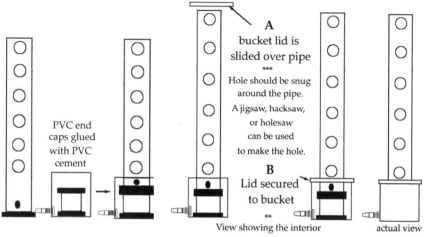

Figure 4.155: Placing a column.   **Figure 4.156: Lid placed over the pipe.**

Within the figures:

PVC end caps glued with PVC cement

A
bucket lid is slided over pipe
***
Hole should be snug around the pipe.
A jigsaw, hacksaw, or holesaw can be used to make the hole.
B
Lid secured to bucket
**
View showing the interior   actual view

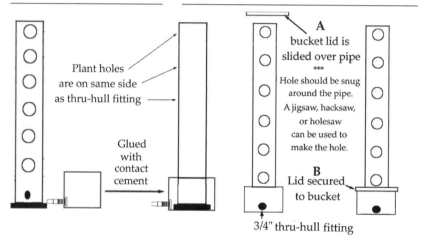

Figure 4.157: Pipe glued to bucket.   **Figure 4.158: Lid over the pipe.**

Within the figures:

Plant holes are on same side as thru-hull fitting

Glued with contact cement

A
bucket lid is slided over pipe
***
Hole should be snug around the pipe.
A jigsaw, hacksaw, or holesaw can be used to make the hole.
B
Lid secured to bucket

3/4" thru-hull fitting

Option B:

1. The end cap of the long pipe is glued to the bottom of the 3-gallon bucket with contact cement.

2. The lids are placed over the tops of the pipes to give a tight fit. Holes can be cut in the centers of the lids with a 4 1/4-inch holesaw, jigsaw, or hacksaw.

3. Four-inch PVC pipes are filled up with medium (i.e. soilless mix). This can also be done after complete setup. Duct tape placed over the holes will prevent the mix from leaking. The mix should be nice and wet before the holes are exposed.

4. The buckets can be placed on top of cement blocks for better drainage.

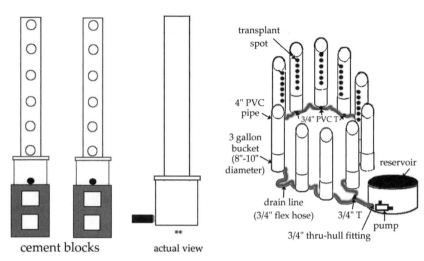

cement blocks   actual view

Figure 4.159 and 4.160: Columns on blocks.

Figure 4.161: Drain line setup is completed.

G. 6 inches of ¾-inch drain hose is attached to each thru-hull fitting. (Figure 4.160)

H. The pipes should be placed in a circle to be 1-foot + plant distance from bulbs in middle. (Figure 4.160)

I. A ¾-inch PVC T is attached to each piece of 6-inch hose. (Figure 4.161)

J. All drain buckets are connected to each other with tubing that is connected to ¾-inch thru-hull fittings. (Figure 4.161) This is like a chain that can be shaped any way that is desired to place plants at optimum light distances. (Figure 4.161)

K. The drain lines of the first two buckets nearest the reservoir will connect to a ¾-inch PVC T and the ¾-inch thru-hull fitting in the reservoir. (Figure 4.161)

Feeder Line Components
L. A long piece of ½-inch poly tubing should be run along the tops of the pipes until it reaches the last one in the circle. A ½-inch PVC T is inserted at the end. (Figure 4.162) Fittings are inserted into main line to let solution run into each pipe. (Figure 4.163)

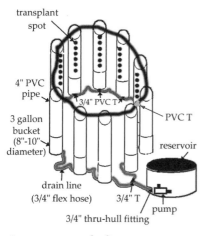

Figure 4.162: Header lines on top.

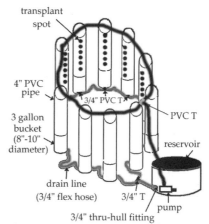

Figure 4.164: Pump is connected.

Figure 4.163: Barbed fitting in pipe.

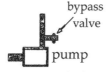

Figure 4.165: Bypass valve location.

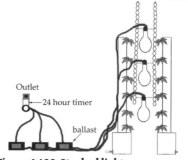

Figure 4.166: Stacked lights.

M. The pump is connected to a piece of poly tubing that reaches the outside of the reservoir. (Figure 4.164)

Option: A bypass valve can be inserted between the pump and the first ½-inch PVC elbow. To insert a bypass valve, a 1-inch chunk is cut out of the ½-inch poly line. Then a ½-inch PVC T is inserted into the cutout section. A 5-inch chunk of ½-inch poly plastic is connected to the ½-inch PVC T, and a lightweight plastic tap is connected to the 5-inch chunk of black poly piece.

Lighting

N. Lights are hung in between the plants without hoods. For example, three to four 400-watt lights (2 to 3 sodiums and 1 halide in middle) can be placed on top of each other in order to illuminate the plants grown in 6-foot high pipe.

Column System D: Top-Feeding Using Plastic Sacks or PVC Pipe

Materials

1. One reservoir for feeding.
2. One reservoir for flushing.
3. Plastic horticulture sacks.
4. Pump.
5. Bypass valve.
6. ½-inch black poly tubing for header lines.
7. ½-inch black poly elbows.
8. ½-inch black poly Ts.
9. ½-inch black poly end caps.
10. ¾-inch flex hos.
11. One bucket per pipe to collect runoff solution.
12. ¾-inch thru-hull fittings.
13. ¾-inch end cap.
14. ⅛-inch tubing for feeder lines.
15. Twine.

Tools

1. Exacto knife.
2. Crescent wrench.
3. Scissors.
4. Hacksaw.

Introduction

This system is for growing small plants with 4-inch PVC or plastic sacks filled with a medium like soilless mix, or 70% perlite / 30% vermiculite. The sacks or pipes are hung from the ceiling with chains or rope. The solution is fed into each pipe and the waste runs to the floor or into a bucket.

Seedlings can be induced to flower when they are 4 to 5 weeks old. Clones can be induced to flower when they are 6 inches tall.

The productive lighting choice is to use three 400-watt lights with 10 to 12 pipes, or two 1,000-watt lights with 28 pipes.

Flat gardens are simpler to setup and maintain on a larger scale.

Plant Holding Components

A. The sacks or pipes will be 4 to 5 feet in height, which allows 6 grow sites per column. Horticulture sacks can be purchased ready-made or they can be made special order by a plastic company. 4-inch PVC pipe is readily available and much easier to find.

B. Plastic horticulture sacks or 4-inch PVC pipe are filled with medium such as soilless mix. Bigger sacks give more area for vegetation to cover. 4 to 6-inch diameter sacks will be fine. If 4-inch PVC is used, 4-inch PVC end caps should be glued to one end of each pipe.

C. Small drain holes should be inserted into the bottoms of the sacks or pipes. With plastic sacks, a nail can make holes. With PVC, a drill and a small $1/8$-inch drill bit can be used for hole making. Now is a good time to soak the mix with plain water. Then the pipes can be topped-up with wet mix because the mix will shrink as it gets wet. The sack can sit in a bucket to collect the water runoff.

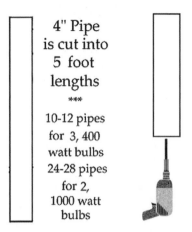

4" Pipe
is cut into
5 foot
lengths

***

10-12 pipes
for 3, 400
watt bulbs
24-28 pipes
for 2,
1000 watt
bulbs

Figure 4.167 and 4.168: PVC pipes.

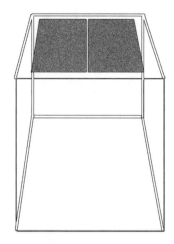

Figure 4.169: Ceiling support.

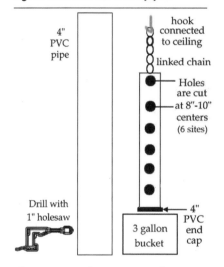

4"
PVC
pipe

hook
connected
to ceiling

linked chain

Holes
are cut
at 8"-10"
centers
(6 sites)

Drill with
1" holesaw

4"
PVC
end
cap

3 gallon
bucket

Figure 4.170 and 4.171: Hung column.

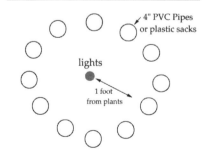

4" PVC Pipes
or plastic sacks

lights

1 foot
from plants

Figure 4.172: Lights and pipe in position.

D. Two ½-inch plywood sheets (or particle board) are nailed into the ceiling to support the system. The plywood sheets are sold as 4x8 sheets. Two sheets will work fine for a 10 to 12 pipe system, or 28-pipe systems in a normal size bedroom.

E. Small holes should be made in each pipe at 8 to 10-inch centers. 8-inch centers would work fine for a 12-pipe system, or 10-inch centers for a 10-pipe system. (Figure 4.170) If PVC pipe is used, a 2-inch holesaw will make a nice cut. (Figures 4.170 and 4.171) If plastic sacks are used, an exacto knife can be used to make a hole slightly larger than the root system of each plant. (Figure 4.171)

F. All sacks or pipes should be hung from hooks that are screwed into the

linked chain

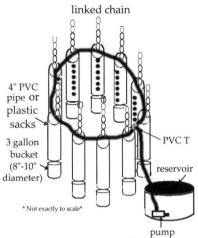

4" PVC pipe or plastic sacks

3 gallon bucket (8"-10" diameter)

PVC T

reservoir

* Not exactly to scale*

pump

Figure 4.173: Header line added.

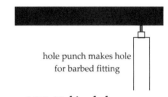

hole punch makes hole for barbed fitting

Figure 4.174: Making holes.

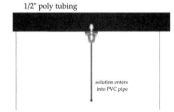

1/2" poly tubing

solution enters into PVC pipe

Figure 4.175: Solution into pipe.

plywood sheets or ceiling studs. If PVC is used, the end cap should be on the bottom. The sacks should be placed in the desired locations. (Figures 4.171 and 4.172)

Feeding and Draining Components

G. Buckets can be placed under each pipe to catch the waste solution. (Figure 4.173)

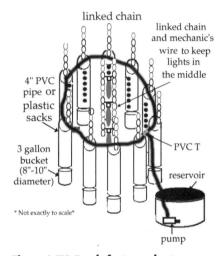

linked chain

linked chain and mechanic's wire to keep lights in the middle

4" PVC pipe or plastic sacks

3 gallon bucket (8"-10" diameter)

PVC T

reservoir

* Not exactly to scale*

pump

Figure 4.176: Ready for transplants.

H. ½-inch hose can be coiled in a circle on top of all of the pipes. It can be drawn through the chain, or tied to rope so that it stays nicely in place. When a circle is made around all of the pipes, a ½-inch PVC T is inserted. (Figure 4.173)

I. The ½-inch PVC T is connected to ½-inch tubing, which is connected to a pump in the bottom of the reservoir. A 20-gallon reservoir such as a 20-gallon garbage can will work. Some growers are picky and would use nothing but a high-end, food-grade product.

J. A small ⅛ to ¼-inch barbed fitting is inserted into the ½-inch main line above each pipe. This is how the pipes will be watered.

Lighting

Lights are hung in between the plants without hoods. For example, three 400-watt lights can be placed on top of each other in order to illuminate the plants grown in sacks.

Feeding

Plants can be fed once a day for fast, productive growth. Plants will grow fine as long as medium does not dry up. Feeding every few days is the easiest way, but growth will be slower than with daily feeding

NFT (Nutrient Film Technique)

With nutrient film technique, plants can be fed with a continuous or intermittent film (using a timer) floating down a trough, PVC pipe, or flood table. The

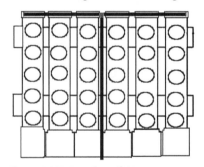

solution travels to the top of a trough through a header line. Then the solution travels down the bottom of the trough where it collects in the reservoir before it is recirculated. Capillary matting can be placed under the trough. Air pumps can be used to aerate the nutrient solution.

Figure 4.177: Top view of NFT.

Automatic thermostatic heat cords can be placed around a reservoir to keep the solution warm. Chillers cool the reservoir.

NFT System A: Sea of Green Using PVC Pipe

Materials

1. 4 to 6-inch PVC pipe.
2. One PVC end cap for each row.
3. One PVC T for each row, less the first and last row.
4. ½-inch poly tubing for header line.
5. Three PVC elbows.

6. One ½-inch poly end cap.

7. One ½-inch poly elbow.

8. ¼-inch feeder lines.

9. ¼-inch connecter fittings.

10. Pump.

11. Bypass valve.

12. Reservoir.

Tools

1. Saw.

2. Sandpaper.

3. Drill.

4. 3½-inch holesaw.

Introduction:

This system is used to grow small plants for the top buds. With this system, the solution goes to the back of the pipes, then it runs down the pipe back into the reservoir. The roots feed from this aerated nutrient solution. A grower can use this system with no medium, or a medium on the bottom of the pipes. Using no medium is the more popular of the two methods becauseit is much cheaper and easier to set up. Feeding every 20 minutes for 2 minutes works well and an hourly timer can be used to keep this constant schedule 24 hours a day, 7 days a week. A medium allows a grower less maintenance with only one daily 10-minute feeding session. Lightweight mediums like soilless mix, perlite, vermiculite or coco fibers can be used.

Bud clusters show Sativa genetics.

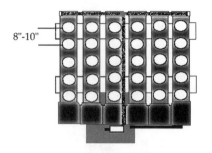

8"-10"

Figure 4.178: 8 to 10-inch spacing.

Figure 4.179: Pipes on 2x4s and blocks.

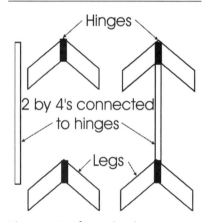

Hinges

2 by 4's connected to hinges

Legs

Figure 4.180: Alternative pipe support.

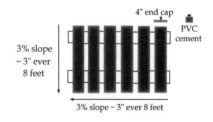

4" end cap

PVC cement

3% slope ~ 3" ever 8 feet

3% slope ~ 3" ever 8 feet

Figure 4.181: Slope is necessary.

Procedure

A. The 4 to 6-inch pipe will be placed on something that supports it. 4-inch pipe is the cheapest. Pipes can be placed upon cement blocks and 2x4s. (Figure 4.179) Or a quick sawhorse can be made with cheap 2x4 wood (i.e. 2 to 3-foot lengths) with hinges that the 2x4 wood slides into. Another 2x4 (ie. an 8-foot length) is placed between the hinges to complete an instant sawhorse. (Figure 4.180)

B. All piping (i.e. 4-inch PVC) should be cut to the desired length.

C. All lengths of large pipe must have end caps attached to the higher ends (i.e. 1 inch higher) that are located at the far side from the reservoir. (Figure 4.181)

D. All large 4-inch pipes (except the first and last pipe) are connected to their neighboring pipe with T-fittings. The first and last pipe are connected with 4-inch elbows. For example, 4-inch pipe will use 4-inch T-fittings. Small pieces of 4-inch pipe are placed between the T-fittings in order to connect the T-fittings and give the desired spacing (i.e. 10-inch centers). Piping and fittings can be glued with PVC cement (for PVC pipe), but the connections will be permanent. The system should not leak without glue if the pipes and fittings are top quality. A little bit of duct tape can be used for securing connections so that disassembly is easy. (Figure 4.182)

Note: One of the 4-inch PVC elbows will have a ¾-inch thru-hull inserted into the bottom for draining. (Figures 4.183 and 4.184)

E. Holes (i.e. 3½ inches) should be cut in the pipe at the desired spacing (i.e. 8 to 12-inch centers). The hole sizes must match the pot sizes to make a custom fit. (Figure 4.185)

F. ½-inch hose is laid down from one end of the PVC pipes to the other end. It can be placed in the middle. (Figure 4.185) This hose is connected to a ½-inch PVC T at the end. Two pieces of hose are connected to the PVC T until they reach the end. ½-inch PVC end caps are attached to the two ends of the hose. (Figure 4.185)

G. A ⅛, ³⁄₁₆, or ¼-inch barbed fitting is inserted into the ½-inch hose above each pipe. A line punch or ¹⁄₁₆-inch drill bit can be used to make the holes in the tubing for the barbed fittings. Holes must be drilled into each pipe so that the barbed fitting goes inside of each pipe. (Figure 4.186)

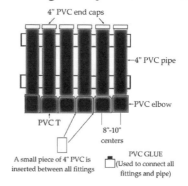

Figure 4.182: Gluing pipes.

Figure 4.183: Drain hole in corner pipe.

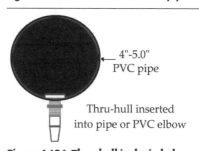

Figure 4.184: Thru-hull in drain hole.

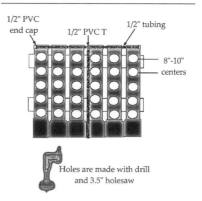

Figure 4.185: Header line in place.

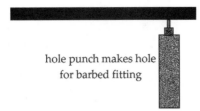

hole punch makes hole
for barbed fitting

Figure 4.186a: Feeder hole.

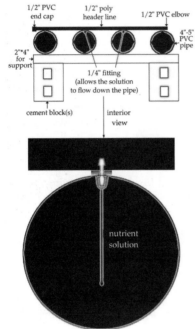

1/2" PVC end cap   1/2" poly header line   1/2" PVC elbow

4"-5" PVC pipe

2"*4" for support

1/4" fitting (allows the solution to flow down the pipe)

cement block(s)   interior view

nutrient solution

Figure 4.186b: Solution delivery.

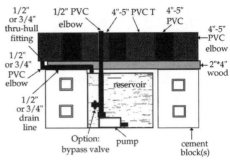

1/2" or 3/4" thru-hull fitting   1/2" PVC elbow   4"-5" PVC T   4"-5" PVC

4"-5" PVC elbow

1/2" or 3/4" PVC elbow

2"*4" wood

reservoir

1/2" or 3/4" drain line

Option: bypass valve   pump   cement block(s)

Figure 4.187: Front view of all parts.

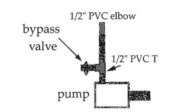

1/2" PVC elbow

bypass valve

1/2" PVC T

pump

Figure 4.188: Bypass components.

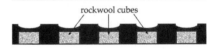

rockwool cubes

Figure 4.189: Cubes in pipe.

3.0" mesh pots with clay, lava rock, 70%perlite/30% vermiculite, or coco fibres

Figure 4.190: Pots in pipe.

H. The ½-inch line that runs parallel down the 4-inch PVC pipes is connected to a ½-inch PVC elbow. The other side of the ½-inch PVC elbow is connected to the pump inside the 20-gallon (or larger) reservoir. (Figure 4.187) A bypass valve can be inserted above the pump to control the flow rate. (Figures 4.187 and 4.188)

I. A ¾-inch piece of flex hose is connected to the ¾-inch thru-hull fitting in the 4-inch PVC pipe. This hose runs to the reservoir. It can go directly to the reservoir or it can be connected to a PVC elbow that goes to the reservoir. (Figure 4.187)

K. Plants in 3-inch rockwool cubes or mesh pots can be placed in the bottom of the pipe.

Bud can flower in an NFT system in as little as 5 to 6 weeks.

NFT System B: V-System Using PVC Pipe
Introduction
NFT works likes this: the solution is pumped from the reservoir along the ½-inch tubing that runs along the back of the 4-inch PVC pipes. Then, the solution leaves the ½-inch tubing through small holes under the tubing. This solution runs along the bottom of each 4-inch PVC pipe until it goes back to the reservoir. The plant feeds from this solution running down the pipe. It is optional to put a medium in the pipe. It makes a garden more trouble free, but adds a higher cost and more work. All the same, since a grower only has to feed once per day, this is much easier on the head than having a garden with pluming running all day if the garden is

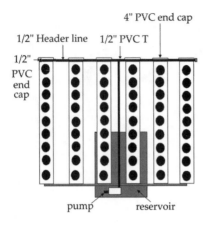

Figure 4.191: NFT top view.

in a risky spot like an apartment. Light weight mediums like soilless mix, perlite, vermiculite or coco fibers could be used. Lightweight mediums that do not compact like clay, lavarock, perlite, vermiculite are good choices to use because compacting mediums like soilless mix and peat moss can be time consumming to re-moisten after they shrink into a compacted mess. They will repel more water than when they have somemoisture.

This system uses two lights and six 4 to 5-inch PVC pipes. The pipes are placed in a V position. This system can produce more volume per square foot than the flat PVC pipe system. The systems described in this section can be used in a 4x5 or 5x8 space.

Tools
1. Saw.
2. Drill
3. One-inch holesaw.
4. 3 to 3½-inch holesaw.
5. Line punch or ¹⁄₁₆-inch drill bit.
6. Hammer.
7. Crescent wrench.

Construction
A. Two 3-foot pieces of 2x4 wood are nailed together with 3 to 4-inch nails to make a 90° angle. (Figure 4.192)

B. Both sides should be cut at a 45° angle at 2 feet high.

C. Three 6-inch pieces of 2x4 are nailed to each side of the V-shaped piece of wood.

D. The *V* is nailed to two 4-foot pieces of 2x4.

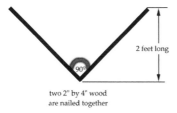

Figure 4.192: V is made.

Figure 4.193: Angle cuts.

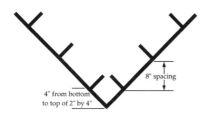

Figure 4.194: 6-inch 2x4s nailed to V.

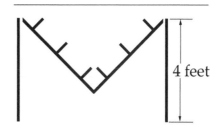

Figure 4.195: V nailed to vertical 2x4s.

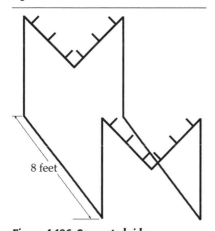

Figure 4.196: Connected sides.

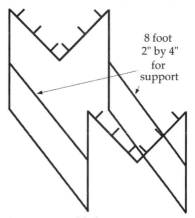

Figure 4.197: Added support.

E. The M-shaped pieces are connected together with two 7 to 8-foot pieces of 2x4.

F. Two 7 to 8-foot pieces of 2x4 are nailed halfway up the lengths for additional support.

G. Two 2x4s are nailed from V to V.

H. Two pieces of 2x4 are nailed to the front and back of the frame for extra support.

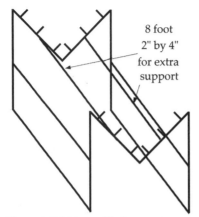

8 foot
2" by 4"
for extra
support

Figure 4.198: More added support.

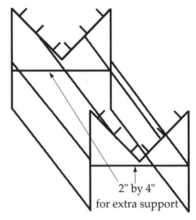

2" by 4"
for extra support

Figure 4.199: Front and back support.

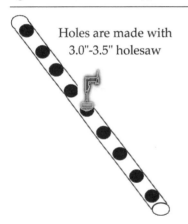

Holes are made with
3.0"-3.5" holesaw

Figure 4.200: Holes for the pots.

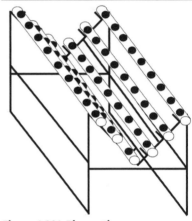

Figure 4.201: Pipe on tiers.

Figure 4.202: Drain hole on the bottom.

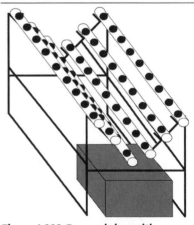

Figure 4.203: Reservoir in position.

I. Holes are cut into the pipes at 8 to 10-inch centers. This makes 9 to 11 sites per 8-foot piece of pipe. Pipes are placed on stand.

Figure 4.204: Thru-hull in the front.

J. A 1-inch holesaw is used to cut holes on the bottom of each pipe for thru-hull fittings. The hole is made in the front.

K. A reservoir is placed under the system.

L. A ¾-inch thru-hull fitting is inserted into each pipe.

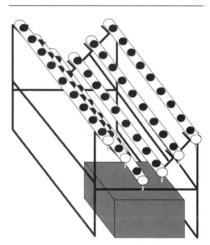

M. 4-inch PVC end caps are connected to both ends of the PVC pipe. PVC glue is used to fasten the end caps.

Figure 4.205: Thru-hulls in all pipes.

N. A piece of ½-inch tubing is connected from the pump to a ½-inch PVC elbow. The elbow should be at the height of the two lowest pipes.

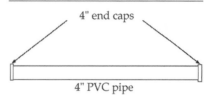

Figure 4.206: End caps on both sides.

O. A ½-inch PVC T is inserted into the end of the line.

P. ½-inch tubing is connected to each side of the PVC T until it reaches the top.

Q. ½-inch end caps are inserted into each end.

R. A line punch, or small drill bit (1/16-inch) is used to make one hole per 4-inch PVC pipe in the ½-inch tubing.

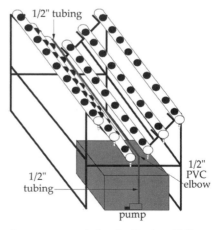

Figure 4.207: Main header line in middle.

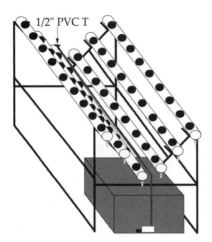

Figure 4.208: 1/2-inch T added.

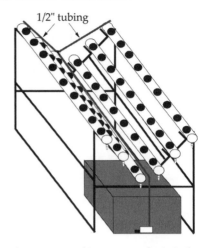

Figure 4.209: Tubing connected to ½-inch T.

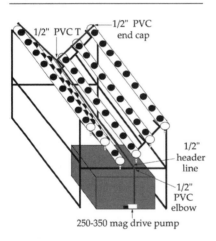

Figure 4.210: End caps attached.

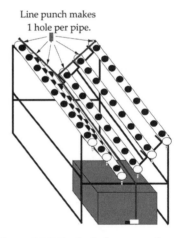

Figure 4.211: Feeder holes are made.

Figure 4.212: Inserted barbed fitting.

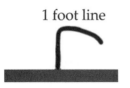

Figure 4.213: Feeder line secured.

Figure 4.214: Hole for feeder line.

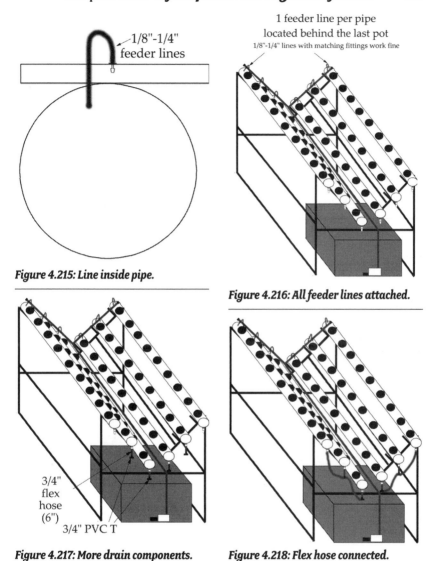

1 feeder line per pipe
located behind the last pot
1/8"-1/4" lines with matching fittings work fine

1/8"-1/4"
feeder lines

Figure 4.215: Line inside pipe.

Figure 4.216: All feeder lines attached.

3/4"
flex
hose
(6")
3/4" PVC T

Figure 4.217: More drain components.

Figure 4.218: Flex hose connected.

S. A connection fitting is inserted into each hole. The fitting can be $\frac{1}{8}$, $\frac{3}{16}$, or $\frac{1}{4}$-inch.

T. A piece of $\frac{1}{8}$, $\frac{3}{16}$, or $\frac{1}{4}$-inch tubing that is 1-foot long is connected to the connection fitting. The size of tubing should match the size of the connection fitting.

U. A hole is drilled into the end of the pipe after the last plant site. The hole should be the same size as the tubing or one size smaller.

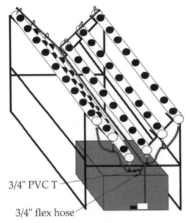

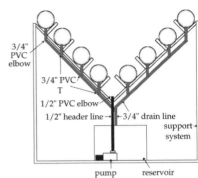

Figure 4.220: Frontal view.

3/4" PVC T

3/4" flex hose

Figure 4.219: Complete hydro system.

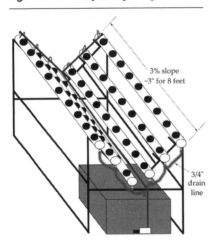

Figure 4.221: 3% slope.

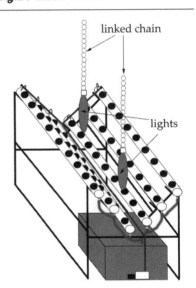

Figure 4.222: Lights in place.

V. The 1-foot line is placed into the hole of the large PVC pipe.

W. Four 6-inch pieces of ¾-inch flex hose are attached to a ¾-inch PVC T on one side and to the lowest four thru-hull fittings on the other side. (Figure 4.217)

X. The highest thru-hulls are connected to the middle thru-hulls with ¾-inch flex hose. The middle thru-hulls are connected to the shortest thru-hulls.

Y. The two lowest ¾-inch PVC Ts are connected to a ¾-inch PVC T. The open end of the PVC T is connected to ¾-inch hose that runs into the reservoir.

Z. The pots go into the pipes. (Figures 4.221 and 4.222)

Aeroponics

Aeroponics is basically hydroponics with a twist. Instead of using a growing medium to anchor roots and run a solution through, the roots are suspended in air and are fed with periodic mistings that are set with a timer. In contrast to top-feeding systems, misters are connected to the ends of the ¼-inch tubing and a stronger pump is used.

A simple aeroponic system can be built by placing 2-inch thick styrofoam on top of a solid, leakproof table. It is best to have the root environment well draining so that roots don't sit in a few inches of slow-moving water.

Another alternative is using PVC pipe or gutter pipe to hold plants in place and to allow the solution to drain back into the reservoir.

One more method is to use a small mesh pot inserted into a larger pail (ie. 5 to 7 gallons).

Aeroponics is cutting-edge horticulture and can take a grower far if he has sound knowledge of hydroponics. Aeroponics can also be of assistance to novice growers for the fact that there is less medium (e.g. clay) to hold salts that hinder growth. However, there are hydroponic methods that use mediums that do not contain too many salts, such as perlite.

A disadvantage of an aeroponic system is the higher cost of the high-powered pump that is necessary to create a highly aerated mist. Another disadvantage is the possibility of large gardens having clogged misters. When misters get clogged during hot hours, there is only so much time to fix the problem before the wilting damage is irreparable.

Hydroponic-Aeroponic Conversion

Many top-feeding hydroponic systems can be converted to aeroponic systems by using a stronger pump, adding a mister for each plant, and changing the position of the mister to feed roots in the air as opposed to top-feeding. Hydroponic systems that use less growing medium will work best, such as those grown in PVC or gutter pipe. Otherwise, flood and drain tables can be converted to aeroponics by putting on a cover such as styrofoam. Hydroponic systems that use very little medium make for an easier conversion.

Aeroponic System A: Sea of Green Using PVC Pipe

Materials

1. One small mesh per plant (i.e. 3½-inch).
2. Two sawhorses (or 2 cement blocks and two 8-foot 2x4s) to support the 8 to 12-foot lengths of pipe.
3. One ⅛-inch threaded barbed fitting per plant.
4. One 1-foot piece of ⅛-inch tubing per plant.
5. One reservoir.
6. Two 4-inch PVC elbow fittings.
7. One 4-inch PVC end cap per 4-inch pipe.
8. Four-inch PVC pipe cut to equal lengths (9 to 10 feet) that are used to hold the plants.
9. One T-fitting for each length of 4-inch pipe.
10. 1,200-gallon per hour (or stronger) pump.
11. Bypass valve.
12. ½-inch black poly tubing for header lines (100-foot roll).
13. Two ½-inch black poly elbows.
14. ½-inch black poly Ts (one for each pipe, minus two).
15. ½-inch black poly end cap for each header line.
16. One 11 to 13 PSI mister per plant.

Tools

1. Drill and 3½-inch hole saw.
2. Knife.
3. Wrench.
4. Handsaw or skillsaw.

Procedure

A. The 4 to 6-inch pipe will be placed on something that supports it like two 2x4s and four cement blocks. (Figure 4.223) A quick sawhorse can be made with cheap 2x4 wood (2 to 3-foot lengths) with hinges that the 2x4 wood slides into. Another 2x4 (an 8-foot length) is placed between the hinges to complete an instant sawhorse. (Figure 4.224)

Close-up bud shot.

B. Two (or more) sawhorses can be used to support the connected pipes. Two sawhorses support an 8 to 12-foot length of 2x4. When the sawhorses are made, the side furthest from the reservoir should be the highest, at equal height. The side nearest the reservoir should be an inch or so lower for every 8-foot length so that the solution drains back into the reservoir.

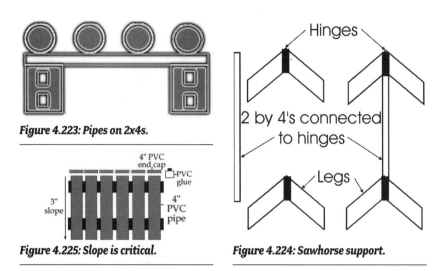

Figure 4.223: Pipes on 2x4s.

Figure 4.225: Slope is critical.

Figure 4.224: Sawhorse support.

C. All piping (of 4-inch PVC) should be cut to the desired length.

D. All lengths of large pipe must be have end caps attached to the higher ends (i.e. 1 inch or higher) that are located at the far side from the reservoir.

E. All large 4-inch pipes (except the first and last pipe) are connected to their neighboring pipe with T-fittings. The first and last pipe are connected with 4-inch elbows. For example, 4-inch pipe will use 4-inch T-fittings. Small pieces of 4-inch pipe are placed between the T-fittings in order to connect the T-fittings and give the desired spacing (such as 10-inch centers). Piping and fittings can be glued with PVC cement (for PVC pipe), but the connections will be permanent.

Note: One of the 4-inch PVC elbows will have a ¾-inch thru-hull inserted into the bottom for draining. (Figure 4.227)

F. Holes of, say, 3½ inches should be cut in the pipe at the desired spacing of 8 to 12-inch centers. The hole sizes must match the pot sizes in order to make a custom fit.

G. Header Line Setup

   1. ½-inch poly tubing should be run along the outside of the pipes until it reaches the end. It should be cut to a length that reaches the middle of the T-fittings and elbow fitting that will be connected to the larger pipe at the shorter end.

The ½-inch poly tubing must have a ½-inch end cap.

2. Another ½-inch poly line will run over the 4-inch T-fittings and 4-inch elbows. This ½-inch tubing will be connected to the other ½-inch poly tubing that runs through the lengths of pipe. All ½-inch tubing should have a ½-inch T-fitting inserted in the middle tubes and ½-inch elbows at the ends. They must be at the desired spacing. (Figure 4.230)

H. Small holes should be punched into the ½-inch header line.

I. Threaded fittings (i.e. ³⁄₁₆, ⅛, ½-inch) should be inserted into each hole.

J. The feeder lines are connected to the fittings. The appropriate sized tubing should be connected to the fittings in the header line. For example, ³⁄₁₆-inch tubing should be connected to a ³⁄₁₆-inch fitting. The tubing should be cut to a length that will reach the larger hole (for the pots) with slack.

K. A mister can be connected to the tubing.

L. The tubing can be drawn through the plant container to the bottom of the plant. (Figure 4.232)

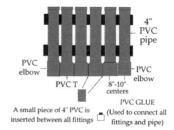

Figure 4.226: Glued pipes.

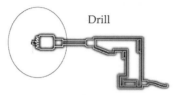

Figure 4.227: Drilling a drain hole.

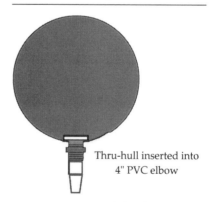

Figure 4.228: Inserted thru-hull.

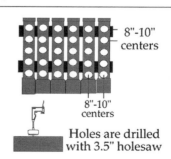

Figure 4.229: Holes for pots.

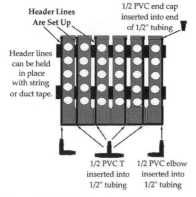

Header Lines
Are Set Up

Header lines
can be held
in place
with string
or duct tape.

1/2 PVC end cap
inserted into end
of 1/2" tubing

1/2 PVC T
inserted into
1/2" tubing

1/2 PVC elbow
inserted into
1/2" tubing

Figure 4.230: Placing header lines.

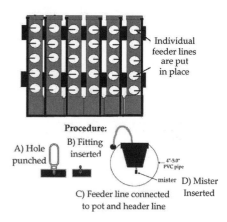

Individual
feeder lines
are put
in place

Procedure:

A) Hole
punched

B) Fitting
inserted

4"-5.0"
PVC pipe

mister D) Mister
Inserted

C) Feeder line connected
to pot and header line

Figure 4.231: Feeder line setup.

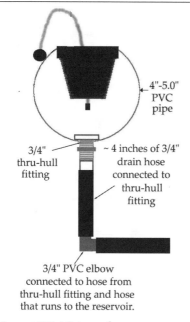

4"-5.0"
PVC
pipe

3/4"
thru-hull
fitting

~ 4 inches of 3/4"
drain hose
connected to
thru-hull
fitting

3/4" PVC elbow
connected to hose from
thru-hull fitting and hose
that runs to the reservoir.

Figure 4.232: Mister under pot.

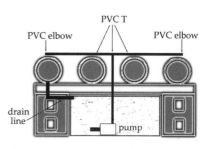

PVC T

PVC elbow

PVC elbow

drain
line

pump

Figure 4.233: Front view of system.

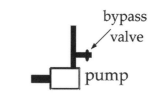

bypass
valve

pump

Figure 4.234: Bypass valve.

M. The outside of the thru-hull fitting in the 4-inch elbow can be connected to ¾-inch hose that leads back to the reservoir.

N. A ½-inch line runs from the pump to the header lines that run along the 4-inch pipes. A ½-inch PVC T is used to connect the lines together.

Recommended Option: A ½-inch poly T should be inserted a few inches above the pump that sits at the bottom of the reservoir. A small piece (say 3 inches) of ½-inch poly tubing is connected to the ½-inch T. A bypass valve should be connected to the small piece of ½-inch tubing in order to control the flow rate.

Feeding

It is easiest to feed the plants with the pump timer running full-time, only during the light hours. But plants can be fed continuously all day and all night. Also, plants can be fed intermittently, such as every 20 minutes for two minutes during the light hours, and once in the middle of darkness.

Finally, plants can be fed at the same intervals for the light and dark hours, too.

Aeroponic System B: V-System Using PVC Pipe and Containers

Introduction

In most cases, this system is used to cultivate small plants for the top buds. Seedlings can be induced to flower at 5 weeks while clones can be induced to flower at 6 inches tall.

Plants are grown in a V shape. This allows for a greater yield than plants that are all at the same height. This system can be constructed cheaply with 2x4 wood and 4-inch PVC pipe.

Like most aeroponic systems, this one is used by experienced growers who can easily troubleshoot the system. A novice grower may want to use the NFT V-system on page 121 or the top-feeding V-system on page 86.

The material list below is described for a common 6-pipe system.

Materials:

1. One small mesh per plant (i.e. 3½ inches).
2. Ten 2x4s to support the 8 to 12-foot lengths of pipe.
3. One ⅛-inch threaded barbed fitting per plant.
4. One-foot piece of ⅛-inch tubing per plant.
5. One reservoir.
6. Six ½-inch PVC end caps.
7. Four-inch PVC pipe cut to equal 9 to 10-foot lengths.
8. Twelve 4-inch PVC end caps.
9. 1,200-gallon per hour (or stronger) pump.

10. Bypass valve.

11. ½-inch black poly tubing for header lines (75 to 100-foot roll).

11. Two ½-inch PVC elbows.

12. Five ¾-inch PVC Ts.

13. Six ½-inch PVC end caps.

14. Six ¾-inch thru-hull fittings

15. Ten feet of ¾-inch flex hose.

16. One 11 to 13 PSI mister per plant.

17. Clay or lavarock to fill each pot.

18. 3 to 3½-inch nails.

Tools

1. Saw.

2. Drill.

3. One-inch holesaw.

4. 3 to 3½-inch holesaw.

5. Line punch or ¹⁄₁₆-inch drill bit.

6. Hammer.

7. Crescent wrench.

System Construction
Frame

A. Two 3-foot pieces of 2x4 wood are nailed together with 3 to 4-inch nails to make a 90° angle. (Figure 4.236)

B. Both sides should be cut at a 45° angle at 2 feet high.

C. Three 6-inch pieces of 2x4 are nailed to each side of the V-shaped piece of wood.

D. The *V* is nailed to two 4-foot pieces of 2x4.

E. The M-shaped pieces are connected together with two 7 to 8-foot pieces of 2x4.

F. The two 7 to 8-foot pieces of 2x4 are nailed halfway up the lengths for additional support.

Transplanted seedlings or clones positioned side by side to utilize light.

Young transplant is thriving in the grow room.

Damping off: weak clone can not handle the wet mix.

Top view of plants that are growing rapidly.

The leaves of this small plant are open to receive light from above.

Healthy plant grown in soilless mix.

Plants are getting more crowded.

The first preflowers are noticeable on this female.

Two pistils next to a broken stalk.

The plant the furthest from the light has more space between plant nodes.

Oscillating fan helps move the air so that air temperature near the plants is more uniform. The fan also helps control temperature in the grow room.

Horizontal hoods are hung with linked chains.

Flowers are becoming noticeable during early flowering.

Plants look bushier because flowers are developing between the nodes.

Fan leaves forming in the bud look long and thin.

The weak plant has no place in a healthy garden. It can be a harbor to pests such as insects.

Small buds are very noticeable at the tops and the nodes.

Close-up showing where buds form at the flower tops and nodes.

The small buds will fuse together.

Plants are trained with wooden stakes to allow leaves and buds more access to light.

Close-up of female pistils.

Those buds have finally covered the stalk on this top.

Wire netting is used to train the limbs on the plant.

String is used to support the weak, lower limbs.

Buds are growing thicker with time.

A carpet of bud.

Training buds is a cheap way to make sure they get sufficient lighting. Buds that stay in the shade will be small.

Bud between bamboo.

View of the lower garden section where light is less plentiful and bud growth is noticeably sparser.

The plant is a heavy consumer of plant food at this stage.

Buds are getting larger and, as buds grow, their odor increases.

Crystals become more apparent as the bud grows.

When a plant has brown hairs and green leaves, the soilless mix should get flushed to ensure that the bud will taste good when it is smoked.

Complete plant is trained with bamboo and mesh.

White pistils are turning brown. A sign that harvest time is soon approaching.

If upward leaf curl does not result in burning tips, there is no need to panic.

Many fan leaves protrude on this variety. In general, a higher fan leaf count means more of a chore when it comes time to manicuring the plant.

Upward leaf curl. If the leaves burn at the tips, the medium must be flushed to remove salt build-up and reduce the risk of over-fertilization.

Harvest time: more brown hairs than white hairs are present.

The maturing bud looks like a maze of hairs with a few small leaves scattered in between.

Plants get light on the sunny side, but the back side is shaded. Rotating plants helps provide optimal light to the complete plant.

Light had been kept at a distance where plants in the entire garden obtain lots of light, yet not to close to avoid them getting too hot.

The garden is full of healthy buds just days away from harvest.

Buds hang to dry on the stalk.

Buds have been dried on the stalk and are now given a final manicure.

The dried buds are largest on top and smallest on the bottom.

At this point, leaves should be cut out.

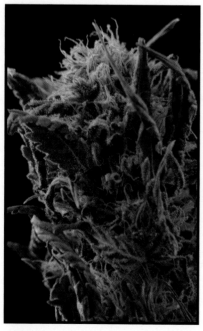

Ripe bud.

The leaves should be cut out and the plant should be sweated in a plastic airtight bag. Then, before it can be smoked or stored, it should be dried again until the stalk cracks.

A view of the entire plant after it has been dried.

Small stalks are separated from the main stalk.

The final manicure. All stalks and leaves have been separated.

The weigh-in.

Time for the tedious pick job.

Dried plant.

The buds have been picked so that they look like a typical stash of grass.

Weighing the plant to know the yield: scales can also be used to weigh homemade fertilizer.

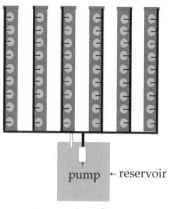

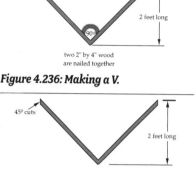

Figure 4.236: Making a V.

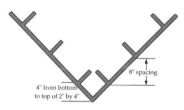

pump ← reservoir

Figure 4.235: Top view of system.

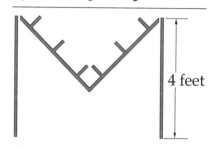

Figure 4.237: Angle cutting.

Figure 4.238: Holders attached.

Figure 4.239: V connected to 2x4s.

G. Two 2x4s are nailed from V to V.

H. Two pieces of 2x4 are nailed to the front and back of the frame for extra support.

I. Holes are cut into the pipes at 8 to 10-inch centers. This is 9 to 11 sites per 8-foot piece of pipe.

J. Pipes are placed on stand.

K. A 1-inch holesaw is used to cut holes on the bottom of each pipe for thru-hull fittings. The hole is made in the front.

L. A ¾-inch thru-hull fitting is inserted into each pipe.

M. 4-inch PVC end caps are connected to both ends of the PVC pipe. PVC glue is used to fasten the end caps.

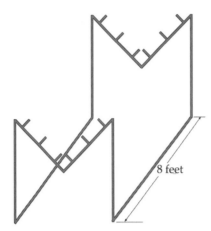

Figure 4.240: Both sides attached.

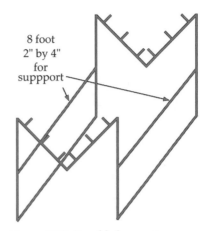

8 foot 2" by 4" for suppport

Figure 4.241: An added support.

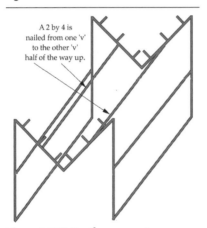

A 2 by 4 is nailed from one 'v' to the other 'v' half of the way up.

Figure 4.242: Another support.

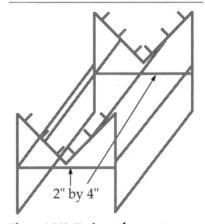

2" by 4"

Figure 4.243: Horizontal support.

Holes are made with 3"-3.5" holesaw

Figure 4.244: Sites are made.

Figure 4.245: Pipe in place.

N. The reservoir is placed under the front.

O. The header line is set up as follows:

   1. A piece of ½-inch tubing is connected from the pump to a ½-inch PVC T.

   2. Two pieces of ½-inch tubing are connected to the ½-inch PVC T. The tubing must reach the highest pipes on each side.

   3. ½-inch PVC elbows are attached to the ends of the tubing.

   4. ½-inch PVC Ts are inserted into the tubing next to the other big pipes.

   5. ½-inch tubing (8 feet) is connected to each ½-inch PVC elbow and ½-inch PVC T.

   6. ½-inch PVC end caps are inserted into the ends of all ½-inch tubing.

P. The feeder line is set up as follows:

   1. A hole is made in the ½-inch tubing next to each plant site using a hole punch.

   2. A threaded fitting is inserted into each line. ⅛ to ³⁄₁₆-inch fittings work fine.

   3. One-foot of ⅛ to ³⁄₁₆-inch tubing is cut for each plant site.

   4. A hole should be drilled into each 3 to 3½-inch mesh pot in the middle of the bottom. The hole

Figure 4.246: Making a drain hole.

Thru-hull inserted

Figure 4.247: Connected thru-hull.

Figure 4.248: Thru-hull fastened.

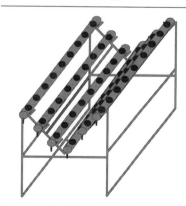

Figure 4.249: All pipes and thru-hulls.

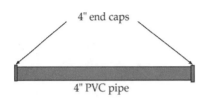

Figure 4.250: End caps at the ends.

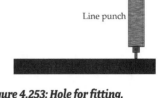

Figure 4.253: Hole for fitting.

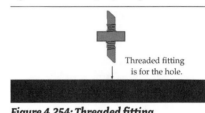

Figure 4.254: Threaded fitting.

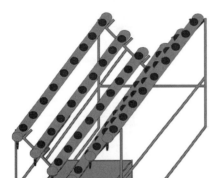

Figure 4.251: Reservoir in front.

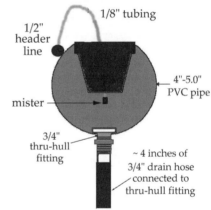

Figure 4.255: Mister position.

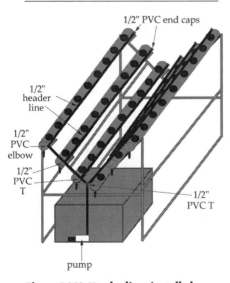

Figure 4.252: Header lines installed.

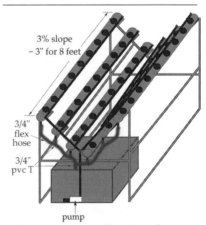

Figure 4.256: Drain lines joined.

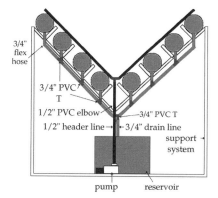

Figure 4.257: System side view.

should be one size smaller than the tubing size to make a tight fit.

5. The 1-foot line is drawn through the hole in the mesh pot. A mister is attached to the tubing.

6. The other end of the 1-foot piece of tubing is attached to the threaded fitting in the ½-inch tubing.

7. A pot can be placed securely in each hole. The mister should be an inch or so from the bottom of the pot.

Q. The drain line is set up as follows:

1. The four lowest ¾-inch thru-hull fittings are connected to ¾-inch PVC Ts with 6-inch pieces of ¾-inch flex hose.

2. The highest thru-hull fittings on each side are connected to the nearest ¾-inch PVC Ts with the flex hose.

3. The lowest and second lowest thru-hull fittings are connected to one another with flex hose.

4. The lowest thru-hulls are connected together with a ¾-inch PVC T.

5. The loose end of the ¾-inch PVC T is connected to flex hose that runs inside the reservoir.

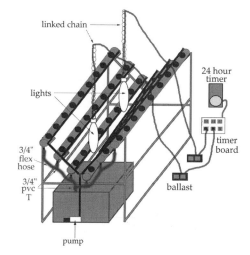

Figure 4.258: Stationary lights.

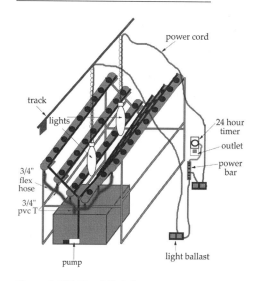

Figure 4.259: Track lighting.

Lighting

R. Two lights can be placed $\frac{1}{3}$ the distance from each end. Two 1,000-watt lights would need to run off of a 220 (240)-volt circuit like a dryer or oven or a 30-amp fuse at the breaker box. (Figure 4.258)

A 1,000-watt light and a 400-watt light, or two 600-watt lights could run on a regular household 15-amp circuit.

Track lighting could be used with 2 lights. (Figure 4.259)

Aeroponic System C: Column System Using PVC Pipe and Containers

Introduction

This system is the fastest, cheapest, and easiest column system to build.

In most cases, this system is used to grow small plants. Seedlings can be induced to flower at 5 weeks old, clones at 6 inches.

Typical uses for this system are 12 pipes at 8-inch centers or 10 pipes at 10-inch centers using three 400-watt lights. Or 28 pipes at 8-inch centers, or 24 pipes at 10-inch centers using two 1,000-watt lights.

But a grower can use half of the pipes described above and double the spacing to grow midsize plants. This system mists roots that are inside of the PVC pipe.

The feeding in this system can be done continually, or every 20 minutes for 2 minutes.

Materials

1. One mesh per plant (i.e. 2 inches).
2. One $\frac{1}{8}$-inch fitting per plant.
3. One piece of $\frac{1}{8}$-inch tubing per plant.
4. One reservoir.
5. Four-inch PVC pipe.
6. Pump.
7. Bypass valve.
8. $\frac{1}{2}$-inch black poly tubing.
9. $\frac{1}{2}$-inch black poly elbows.
10. $\frac{1}{2}$-inch black poly Ts.
11. $\frac{1}{2}$-inch black poly end caps.
12. $\frac{3}{4}$-inch flex hose.

Large, productive commercial setup.

13. One 3-gallon bucket per pipe.

14. ¾-inch thru-hull fittings.

15. ¾-inch end cap.

16. 6ml black poly.

17. Twine.

18. Contact cement.

19. 11 to 13 PSI misters.

Tools

1. Drill and 1-inch holesaw.

2. Exacto knife.

3. Crescent wrench.

4. Custom-sized holesaw (i.e. 3½ inches).

5. Handsaw or skillsaw.

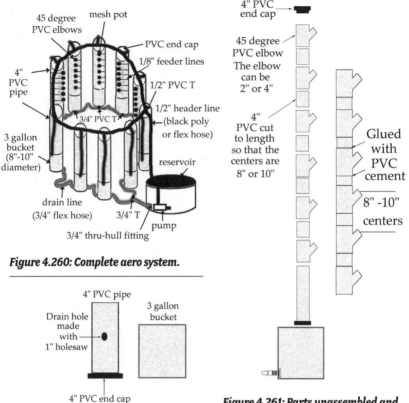

Figure 4.260: Complete aero system.

Figure 4.262: Drain hole.

Figure 4.261: Parts unassembled and parts assembled.

Procedure

Plant-Holding Components

A. Choosing the desired pipe is the first step: 4 to 8-inch PVC is a good. The 4-inch is cheapest, but larger pipe is easier to use because there is more room for the roots. To keep things simple, these instructions are with 4-inch PVC:

Option A:
In this example, 45° 4-inch PVC elbows are used for the plant holders. (Figure 4.261)

Option B:
This easier option is to buy the pipe with the plant holders built into the plastic; they come with plant holders on one side for indoor systems.

B. All 4-inch piping should be cut into small pieces (i.e. 6 inches) so that when they are glued with the 45° PVC elbows the distance between plants will be 8 to 10-inch centers. (Figure 4.261) The 4-inch piping is glued with PVC cement to the 4-inch PVC elbows so that the space is 8 to 10-inch centers.

C. The tops of the pipes will have 4-inch PVC end caps attached loosely to the top to keep out light. The cap should be able to be removed easily. (Figure 4.261)

D. One piece of 4-inch PVC should be cut at a height of a few inches above the buckets. A 4-inch end cap should be glued to the bottom with PVC glue.

E. A hole should be made just below the height of the 3-gallon bucket to drain the solution. (Figure 4.262) The buckets should have a diameter less than the center spacing of 8 to 10 inches.

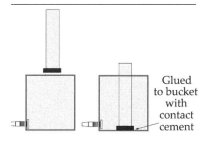

1
Holes are cut
into buckets
with 1" holesaw

2
3/4" thru-hull
fitting inserted
into bucket

Figure 4.263: Bucket drain hole.

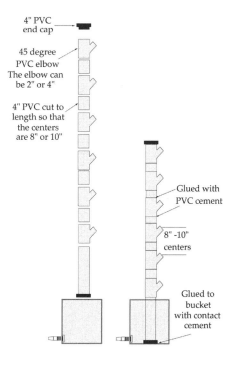

4" PVC
end cap

45 degree
PVC elbow
The elbow can
be 2" or 4"

4" PVC cut to
length so that
the centers
are 8" or 10"

Glued with
PVC cement

8"-10"
centers

Glued to
bucket
with contact
cement

Figure 4.266: Parts unassembled and parts assembled.

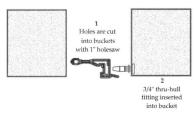

Glued
to bucket
with
contact
cement

Figure 4.264: Contact cementing.

B
Lid secured
to bucket

Figure 4.265: Lid over pipe.

Drain Components

F. Each bucket at the base of the piping should have one hole made about 2 inches from the bottom on each side using a 1-inch holesaw for ¾-inch thru-hull fittings that will be inserted into each hole. (Figure 4.263)

G. The 4-inch PVC pieces (from step D) can be glued to the bottoms of each bucket with contact cement. The placement in the bucket should be dead center. (Figure 4.264)

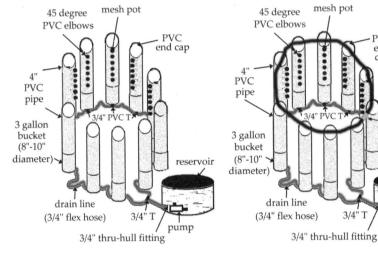

Figure 4.267: Drainage setup.

Figure 4.268: Header line on top.

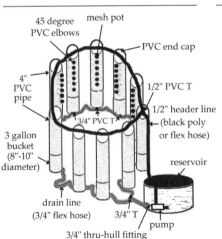

Figure 4.269: Pump connected.

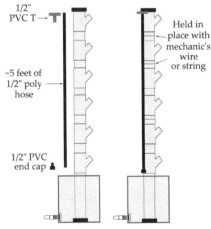

Figure 4.270: Vertical header lines.

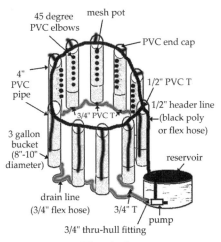

45 degree PVC elbows — mesh pot

PVC end cap

4" PVC pipe

1/2" PVC T

1/2" header line
(black poly or flex hose)

3/4" PVC T

3 gallon bucket (8"-10" diameter)

reservoir

drain line (3/4" flex hose)

3/4" T

pump

3/4" thru-hull fitting

Figure 4.271: All header lines.

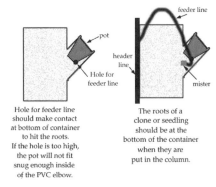

feeder line

pot

header line

Hole for feeder line

mister

Hole for feeder line should make contact at bottom of container to hit the roots. If the hole is too high, the pot will not fit snug enough inside of the PVC elbow.

The roots of a clone or seedling should be at the bottom of the container when they are put in the column.

Figure 4.272: Line through PVC.

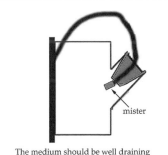

mister

The medium should be well draining for top-feeding in the column. Clay, lava rock and perlite are safe choices.

Figure 4.274: Line through pot.

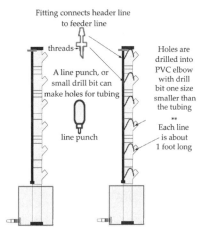

Fitting connects header line to feeder line

threads

A line punch, or small drill bit can make holes for tubing

line punch

Holes are drilled into PVC elbow with drill bit one size smaller than the tubing

**
Each line is about 1 foot long

Figure 4.273: Installing feeder lines.

H. Each bucket lid should have a hole made into it to fit around the pipe. The lid will add extra support to the pipes and make for less water loss through evaporation. The lid can be placed on the bucket when the glue is dry. Holes can be made with a 4¼-inch holesaw, hacksaw, or jigsaw.

I. The columns can be glued with PVC cement to the 4-inch pipe. (Figure 4.266) The columns can be on the same side with or opposite side from the thru-hull fittings.

J. The pipes should be placed in a circle to be 1-foot + plant distance from bulbs in middle. (Figure 4.267)

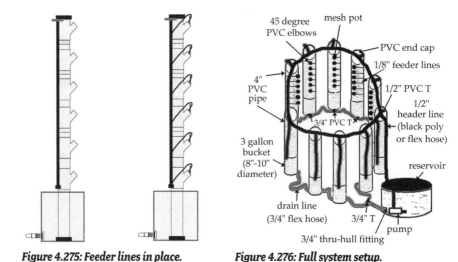

Figure 4.275: Feeder lines in place.   *Figure 4.276: Full system setup.*

K. Take 6 inches of ¾-inch drain hose and attach it to each thru-hull fitting. (Figure 4.267)

L. A ¾-inch PVC T is attached to each piece of 6-inch hose. (Figure 4.267)

M. All drain buckets are connected to each other with tubing that is connected to ¾-inch thru-hull fittings. (Figure 4.267) This is like a chain that can be shaped any way that is desired to place plants at optimum light distances. (Figure 4.267)

N. The first bucket nearest the reservoir will connect to the ¾-inch thru-hull fitting in the reservoir. (Figure 4.267)

Feeder Line Components

O.   1. A long piece of ½-inch poly tubing should be run along the tops of the pipes until it reaches the last one in the circle.

2. A ½-inch PVC T is inserted at the end. (Figure 4.268)

3. The open end of the ½-inch PVC T is connected to a line that runs to the bottom of the reservoir. A 20-gallon reservoir will do. (Figure 4.269)

4. The main line is cut at each pipe, and a ½-inch PVC T is installed for each length of vertical pipe. (Figure 4.270)

5. The PVC T is connected to pieces of ½-inch poly tubing that run down the

sides of the large piping to a height just above the top of the reservoir. (Figure 4.271)

6. The poly tubing is connected to ½-inch PVC end caps.

7. Holes are punched and an appropriate threaded fitting is inserted, such as ⅛-inch fittings for ⅛-inch lines. One fitting is used for each plant.

8. Lines are cut to a length that reaches each plant container with a little slack, and inserted into the connection fittings. There are two options. (Figures 4.272 and 4.273 or 4.274 and 4.275)

8. Misters are inserted in the ends of the tubing.

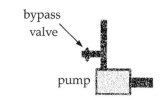

Figure 4.277: Pressure control.

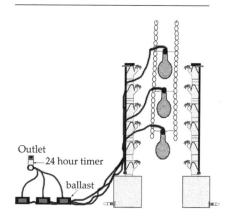

Figure 4.278: Three stacked lights.

P. The pump is connected to the ½-inch poly tubing that reaches the bottom of the reservoir. (Figure 4.276)

Option: A bypass valve can be inserted between the pump and the first ½-inch PVC elbow. To insert a bypass valve:

1. A 1-inch chunk is cut out of the ½-inch poly line.

2. A ½-inch PVC T is inserted into the cut out section.

3. A 5-inch chunk of ½-inch poly plastic is connected to the ½-inch PVC T.

4. A lightweight plastic tap is connected to the 5-inch chunk of 5-inch black poly piece.

Lighting

Q. Lights are hung in between the plants without hoods.

For example, three to four 400-watt lights (two to three sodiums and one halide in middle) can be placed on top of each other to illuminate the plants grown in ten to twelve 6-foot high pipes.

Feeding

R. It is easiest to feed the plants with the pump timer running full-time only during the light hours, with an injection or two in the middle of the dark hours.

But plants can be fed continuously all day and all night. Also, plants can be fed intermittently every 20 minutes for 2 minutes, or for 30 seconds every 2 to 5 minutes during all hours.

More detailed feeding options and instructions are provided in chapter 4.

Soilless Mix Systems

Billy Bob's Organic Hydroponic System

Introduction

This type of system is very popular among growers. Soilless mix is placed in a pot and plants are given water with fertilizer on a regular basis.

Small pots (1 to 3 gallons) can be used for growing smaller plants while large pots can be used for growing larger plants. Growing larger plants is less maintenance because there is less transplanting, less plants are needed for each crop, a smaller number of plants is faster to hand feed, and it is easier to remember to water a plant if there are fewer plants to water. Soilless mix is unquestionably the most versatile horticultural medium. It comes under trade names such as Sunshine Mix and Jiffy Mix.

With this system, a grower can use one of 3 feeding options:

A. Feeding when the mix begins to dry out.

B. Feeding once a day with 20% runoff waste.

C. Continuous feeding.

Feeding could be as minimal as once a week, such as when the medium begins to dry out. Soilless mix is best used to keep the workload down because it retains a lot of moisture and nutrients between periodic feedings (ie. feeding once a week). Immediately after it is daylight or when lights start up is a good time to periodically saturate this medium.

Feeding daily with run-off waste is the easiest way to get high production. This will allow the plant adequate access to nutrients, water, and air to the roots. Since the solution is delivered once a day, the grower can leave the grow room without any worry of damaging water leaks than can occur in hydroponic systems that irrigate at regular intervals or continuously.

Healthy cannabis in decent growing medium.

Nevertheless, if a plant in soilless mix is fed daily or continuously with a top-feeding hydroponic system, plant growth will be much faster than periodic feeding. However, flow rate is critical with Sunshine Mix. If the flow is too fast, water will form puddles and overflow out of the containers.

With soilless mix, continuous feeding works best with slow feeding and large containers. Putting 2 quart (or litre) per hour drippers in the ends of the feeder tubing or slowing the flow to the header line with an open bypass valve will keep the flow rate slow. Drippers come in all sizes for the individual feeder lines.

Another way to run solution through soilless mix is to set an intermittent timer to operate for a couple of minutes at a time, several (say, six) times per day.

Easy Perpetual Harvesting

A grower can use one room for vegetative growth and one for flowering. The vegetative room can be about ½ to ⅔ the size of the flower room. The grower can cut clones from plants in the vegetative room before they are induced to flower, then the plants can go into the flower room. When the clones root, they can be transplanted into 5-gallon pots that go into the vegetative room until the next crop is harvested. This cycle is easy and very low maintenance.

Materials

1. Means of Solution Collecting Under the Buckets

Option A: Commercial plastic flood table(s); they come in sizes like 3x4, 4x4, and 4x8.

Option B: Homemade flood table(s):
    1. One to two 4x8 sheets of ¾-inch plywood.
    2. Two 4-foot pieces of 1x2-inch wood for each sheet.
    3. Two 8-foot pieces of 1x2-inch wood for each sheet.
    4. 6ml black poly plastic.
    5. Seventeen feet of 10-foot wide plastic.

Option C: Plant dishes.

2. Sawhorses to support tables.
3. One 5-gallon bucket for each flood table, to catch runoff solution.
4. One or two bales (3.8 cubic foot / bale; bales are usually found in this or 2 cubic foot sizes) of soilless mix: Sunshine #2 mix, Pro-Mix, or Jiffy Mix. Note: one 3.8 cubic foot bale fills about ten 5-gallon containers.
5. 2 to 20 buckets (or 2 to 20 nursery pots). Smaller gallon buckets (such as 1 to 3-gallon sizes) are good for growing a large number of small plants. Larger containers (such as 5 to 20-gallon buckets) are good for growing a small number of large plants. Both methods are effective. (Figures 4.279, 4.281, and 4.283 show various growing strategies.)
6. Fertilizing materials. Chapter 5 discusses feeding and formulas.

Setting Up

A. The soilless mix is placed into the buckets. A tarp should be laid down for placing and breaking up the chunks of soilless mix.

B. Several drainage holes (up to 75% hole space, meaning that only 25% of the bottom will be showing plastic) should be inserted into the bucket bottoms, using a sharp knife, unless you are using nursery containers with premade holes.

C. The containers with mix can be placed on a flood table with a bucket placed under each table to catch the runoff. Buckets go under the hole in the flood table to capture the wasted nutrient solution. Alternatively, plant dishes can go under each pot to collect the waste from going onto the floor. If plant dishes are used, the solution should be removed from every dish after the feeding so that the bottom roots don't sit in stagnant solution. (Figures 4.281 and 4.287)

The mix in this program is organic hydroponic quality; to qualify in the soilless mix category, a formula must be less than 10% inorganic soil. This formula is much more than 90% soilless. The organic peat, gypsum, dolomite lime, and perlite all qualify as soilless.

The buckets should be filled to about 1 inch from the top.

The mixture in the buckets should be watered until it gets a good soaking.

D. Plants can now be transplanted into the mix.

E. Feeding

With soilless mix, a grower can feed anytime. But, the mix should never become dry and compacted. Daily feeding gives faster growth than feeding at longer intervals like every three days or once a week.

Option A: When mix begins to dry up (Lazy Man's Method)

This is the easiest way to feed. A grower applies water with fertilizer every few days. A grower can apply ½ strength fertilizer every feeding. Organic fertilizer will produce "organic hydroponic bud," and chemical fertilizer produces "hydroponic quality bud." Some companies have specific formulas and instructions for soilless mix, such as General Hydroponics. A safe rule would be to have 10 to 20% waste running through each pot after each feeding. An added option is to

4 foot fluorescent light fixture with 2 tubes

1 gallon pots with plant dishes   cement block

Figure 4.279: Simple garden: pots, dishes, plants, mix, lights, and blocks.

1 gallon pots with plant dishes

Figure 4.280: Fluorescent lights carefully placed on cement blocks.

flush the mix every month with a large dose of plain water.

Note: If the pots are in plant dishes, the solution should be sucked out of each plant dish with a shop vac about 30 minutes after the feeding. If the solution is not sucked out, the plant may spread its bottom feeder roots into the solution of the plant dish. This can alter its feeding routine and cause nutrient deficiencies.

Option B: Daily
This method allows plants to grow rapidly because daily feeding draws in plant food and air to the roots. A grower can apply ½ strength fertilizer every feeding. A safe rule would be to have 10 to 20% waste running through each pot. Once a week, the mix can be flushed with a large dose of plain water. Or a grower can apply ½ strength fertilizer for one feeding, then plain water every second feeding. This pattern can be repeated until plants are 2 weeks before harvest.

The next few pages show the set-ups for three different size spaces.

System Sizes
Billy Bob's Basic
Introduction
The Billy Bob Basic is for growing small plants for nice tops.

A. 24 seedlings can be started under one 4-foot fluorescent fixture.

B. 5 to 6 plants can occupy all of the space under one 4-foot fluorescent light fixture during the flowering cycle. Seedlings or clones can be induced to flower with a 12 hour on / 12 hour off light cycle. Seedlings are induced at 4 to 5 weeks old, clones at 6 inches high.

Notes: One fixture could be used to start 24 seedlings and two fixtures could be used for flowering. One fixture could produce 1 to 3 ounces per crop. Using three fixtures, one for veg and two for flower could yield 2 to 7 ounces every 6 to 11 weeks in a closet, depending on the strain.

Billy Bob's One Lighter
Introduction
This system is used to grow 4 plants around a single light.

If a grower wants midsize plants, a 400-watt halide, a 400-watt sodium, or 200-watt compact fluorescent will work.

If a grower wants midsize to large plants, a 600-watt metal halide (or sodium) or 1,000-watt halide (sodium) is fine.

Figure 4.281: Hood for vegetative growth.   *Figure 4.282: Hoodless flowering option.*

Vegetative Growth
A grow light with hood can be placed above the plants during vegetative growth.

Flowering
A grow light without a hood can be placed in between all 4 plants during flowering. Plants can be rotated so that they all get illuminated.

If midsize plants are the objective, they can be induced to flower when they are 2 to 3 feet high.

If large plants are the objective, they can be induced to flower when they are 3 to 4 feet high.

Billy Bob's Full Bedroom
Introduction
This system can be used to fill up a typical bedroom with midsize to large plants. A grower could grow 9 large plants with this system or 16 midsize plants. The buckets can be placed directly on the floor, in plant dishes, or on top of a flood table. (Figures 4.283 and 4.287 show the options.) If plants go on the floor, there should be a tarp or black plastic on the floor because the solution can make a little mess if it runs onto a carpet.

Vegetative Growth
Two 400-watt grow lights with hoods can be placed above the plants during vegetative growth. (Figure 4.283)

Flowering
Four stationary grow lights can be placed in between all 9 plants during flower-

Figure 4.283: Nine plant setup.   *Figure 4.284: Four lights during flower.*

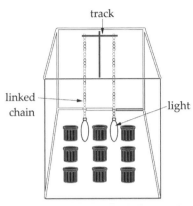

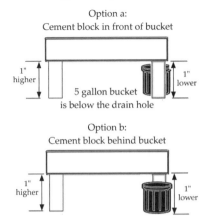

Figure 4.285: Track and two lights.

Figure 4.286: Recovery bucket.

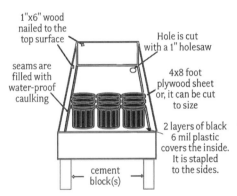

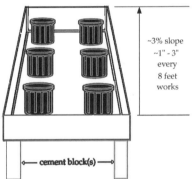

Figure 4.287: Buckets on table.

Figure 4.288: Room for spacing.

ing. (Figure 4.284) They can be rotated so that they all get illuminated. Or two lights and a track can be used. (Figure 4.285)

If midsize plants are the objective, they can be induced to flower when they are 2 to 3 feet high.

If large plants are the objective, they can be induced to flower when they are 3 to 4 feet high.

System Automation Options
Option A: Flood and Drain Add-On
Instead of feeding the plants periodically from the top, a grower can feed the plants by flooding and draining the bottom roots on a flood table when they

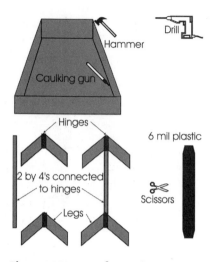

Figure 4.289: Room for spacing.

reach the bottom. The flood table can have a layer (e.g. 1 inch) of a medium like perlite. Or the roots can run freely on the flood table if they have the light blocked using non-toxic reflectix insulation. The pots would have to fit snug into the reflectix to block out the light.

The plants will adjust and roots will feed while growing out the bottoms of the containers. This will be more productive than regular feeding. Plants will no longer need to be fed from the top. The bottom roots will form a thick matt along the flood table. These bottom roots search for food under these new conditions.

Adding this flood and drain option is possible during any part of the program. Constructing the flood and drain system is described on page 49.

Option B: Top-Feeding Add-On

Plants can be fed periodically or continuously with top-feeding. For organic fertilizers, ¼-inch lines are recommended to feed the plants. Plants can be top-fed in the soilless mix, or they can be transplanted into a larger container of a different grow medium, such as clay, and then top-fed from there. Top-feeding details and full setup are explained elsewhere in this chapter. If a grower cannot afford a pump to top feed the plants, the drip system can be used. The construction of the drip system is described on pages 159 to 167. But a $40 investment for a 250 to 350-gallon per hour mag-drive pump is a better option because the solution is delivered faster. Not only is life easier, but slow dripping systems have greater potential to develop clogs in the system than a pumping system that uses a little more force, especially with organic fertilizers.

Option C: Drip-Watering System

Hand watering is a relatively quick and cheap way to go. However, installing a drip system (with or without a computer timer) may allow for easy living. With a drip system, gravity causes liquid to flow from a high elevation downward into

Big buds in this professional garden.

the pots. Hand-feeding is recommended for the beginner, to develop a more hands-on, personal feel to nutrient solution volumes. If the proper amounts of solution are given so that the mix stays gets saturated, the results are respectable. Normally, a few quarts per plant is plenty for plants in 1 to 5-gallon containers, if they are watered before they get too dry. Also, getting close to the plants allows for bug inspections, dead leaf picking, and leaf stroking.

Materials

1. Twenty gallon plastic garbage can for larger rooms, 10-gallon can for smaller rooms. Any size can be used in order to hold the adequate amount of solution (i.e. 2 quarts).

2. ³⁄₄-inch thru-hull fitting with O-ring.

3. Tap (for turning off and on).

4. PVC fitting with a ³⁄₄-inch threaded female end and a ½-inch end for the to fiton the polybutylene tubing.

5. ½-inch PVC end cap.

6. ⅛-inch fittings to plug into header line (one for each plant).

7. Twenty feet of ½-inch polybutylene tubing (or as much as needed).

8. Fifty feet of ⅛-inch polybutylene tubing.

9. Silicone.

10. Inline filter unit and filter with ¾-inch threads (male and female).

11. Computerized water timer (optional).

12. Support system for the garbage can, as high as possible (to be placed in a corner of the room). A very tall stool on top of a platform would be suitable.

1"
holesaw

Figure 4.290: Hole is cut.

13. Sandpaper for plastic (100 to 300 coarse).

14. Small C-clamp (optional).

15. Hole punch for ⅛-inch fittings into header line.

16. Teflon tape.

Tools

1. Drill.

2. One-inch holesaw.

3. A small drill bit (less than ⅛-inch).

4. Handsaw.

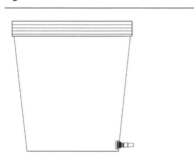

Figure 4.291: Inserted thru-hull fitting.

SetUp

A. A 1-inch hole is drilled into the side of the garbage can with a 1-inch holesaw. The hole should be 2 to 3 inches from the bottom.

B. Insert the ¾-inch hull-thru fitting into the 1-inch hole. The O-ring is on the inside of the can, and the threads are on the outside of the can.

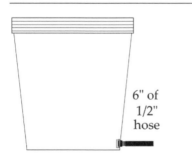

6" of
1/2"
hose

Figure 4.292: Hose connected.

Option A:

A 6-inch piece of ½-inch tubing can be connected the end of the ¾-inch thru-hull fitting.

Option B:

1. The fitting should be cut at the end of the threads located furthest from the garbage can. This cut should be vertical and uniform. The plastic particulate must be sanded before screwing the tap on. Teflon tape can be placed on the threads to prevent leaks.

2. The inline filter is connected. (Figure 4.294) An option is to install a computerized timer to the inline filter. (Figure 4.295)

3. A ½-inch PVC fitting with standard female threads is fastened to the inline filter or computer timer. (Figure 4.296)

4. A 6-inch piece of ½-inch tubing is attached to the ½-inch PVC fitting.

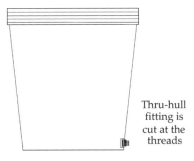

Thru-hull fitting is cut at the threads

Figure 4.293: Threads are cut.

C. A ½-inch *on / off* tap is attached to the ½-inch tubing.

D. The bucket is placed on top of a high stool. (Figure 4.298)

E. The ½-inch tubing is extended diagonally across the room until it reaches the far end corner of a flood table and rests on the surface. The ½-inch tubing should be gently connected to the last fitting so that it is secure yet allows for easy removal of the line to clean the filter. This should hold sufficiently, but a small C-clamp may be used for extra safety. (Figures 4.299 and 4.300)

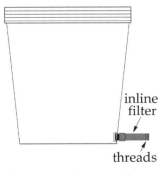

inline filter

threads

Figure 4.294: Filter attached.

F. The end of the ½-inch tubing is cut and a ½-inch end cap is inserted. That joint may be C-clamped. (Figures 4.299 and 4.300)

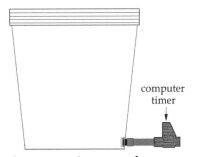

computer timer

Figure 4.295: Timer secured.

G. Somewhere along the lower elevated part of the header line (but higher than the containers), holes should be punched into the line. The number of holes should be equal to the number of plant containers.

H. Small holes are drilled into the tops of the containers (above the mix) for the ⅛-inch tubing to be inserted snuggly, or the tubing can be placed into alligator stakes. If too many holes are made by accident, plugs can be used to fill them.

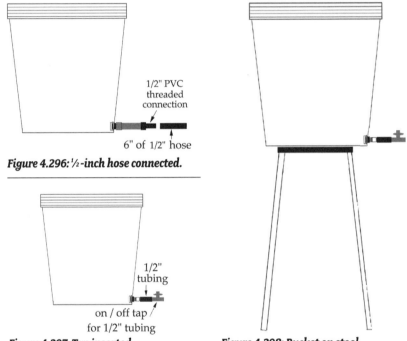

1/2" PVC threaded connection

6" of 1/2" hose

Figure 4.296: ½-inch hose connected.

1/2" tubing

on / off tap for 1/2" tubing

Figure 4.297: Tap inserted.

Figure 4.298: Bucket on stool.

buckets with plant dishes

1/2" PVC end cap

Figure 4.299: Header line placed over the buckets in plant dishes.

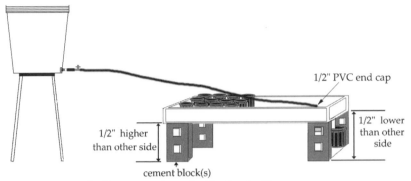

1/2" PVC end cap

1/2" lower than other side

1/2" higher than other side

cement block(s)

Figure 4.300: Header line runs to the end of the flood table.

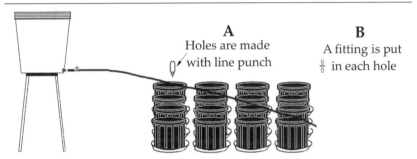

A
Holes are made with line punch

B
A fitting is put in each hole

Figure 4.301: One hole per bucket is made in the header line for the feeder lines.

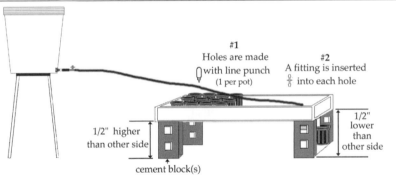

#1
Holes are made with line punch (1 per pot)

#2
A fitting is inserted into each hole

1/2" higher than other side

1/2" lower than other side

cement block(s)

Figure 4.302: Connecting the feeder lines to each pot.

I. The ½-inch tubing is linked between each individual ⅛-inch fitting from the header and each individual container hole, without leaving too much slack. Option: Drippers can be inserted into the end of each feeder line to control the flow rate.

J. If there are any leaks in the polybutylene after testing (such as leaks in the joints), silicone can be used to seal them. Silicon must be applied to dry tubing

Figure 4.303: Hole or alligator stake holds the feeder line.

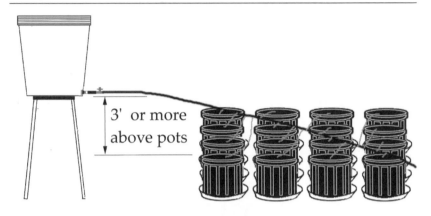

Figure 4.304: Complete setup of pots in plant dishes.

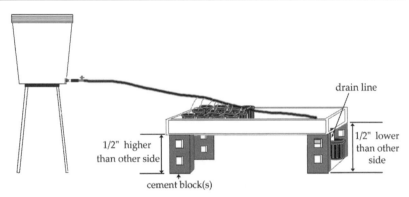

Figure 4.305: Complete assembly of buckets on a flood table.

and it must be allowed to dry. Chances are that if there is a leak, it would only be the odd drop of liquid and not a big deal.

K. As plants get larger and need to be spaced out, more ⅛-inch tubing will be needed to replace some of the existing tubing. Extensions or longer tubing can solve this problem. Using tubing extensions is the easier choice. An exacto knife is used to cut away the old tubing from the fittings in the line.

Drip System Maintenance

This drip system will be trouble-free when plain water is passed through the tubing.

Figure 4.306: Caulking seals cracks.

Some fertilizers, such as bat guano and Sea mix, water with particulate, and other forms of debris can clog the inline filter, ⅛-inch fittings, or ½-inch tubing. However, many fertilizing mixes will not clog the lines. The drip system can be carefully monitored so that disasters, such as plants going without solution, do not occur. The filter can be cleaned often by rinsing it with plain water. Removing the ½-inch end cap and flushing the system with plain water on a regular basis avoids problems.

Figure 4.307: Extending tubing.

Figure 4.308: Extended tubing.

Small tubing may get clogs. Blowing or sucking into the ends of ⅛-inch end tubing helps remove clogs. But if that is necessary, a flush of the system is also necessary.

If the computer timer is part of the program, it should be set to run for plenty of time, so that it will not shut off during the drip process.

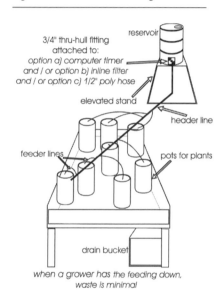

Figure 4.309: Schematic drip system.

Using the computer is a risky business, because it may be used when nobody is home. Why else would it be needed? If premises are vacated, electronic malfunctions, battery failure, clogs in the system, or fluke leaks are all possible.

Going without the computer and taking advantage of a drip system is beneficial. The entire two-room system offers the opportunity to take up to five days off at a time without missing a feeding once watering frequencies are known. Since raising lights, cleanup work, misting, picking dead leaves, bending plants, checking for bugs, checking timers, etc., go along with the job, any more than a few days off is foolish. Freedom is an advantage of this cultivation system because maintenance can be minimal. If a grower is keen, daily feeding maintenance will get a larger yield in less time. If a grower is lazy or does not have the time, feeding and garden maintenance can be done on the same day every few days. Most other sophisticated hydroponic systems have greater potential for error such as leaks and nutrition problems.

The disadvantage of a drip system is that the solution drains into a waste bucket, which then must be manually returned to the reservoir. This manual step can be eliminated when a top-feeding system is built. The top-feeding system recirculates the solution so that the feeding can be effortless, since all feeding maintenance is done in one bucket. The top-feeding system is shown in complete detail starting on page 66.

Making a Top-Quality Mix for the Plants

A quality homemade mix can be made with peat moss, forest compost, or prepared with a soilless mix that is purchased from the store.

Store-bought Preparation

Store-bought goods are easier to work with because the pH is at the desired level and it is mixed with perlite and / or vermiculite, lime, and other goodies. On the other hand, homemade mixes are a lot cheaper, often less than half the price. Organic recipes for soilless mix are described on pages 167 to 174.

When soilless mix is purchased, it is sterilized and has a pH that needs no further adjusting. However, forest compost and peat moss can be substituted for soilless mix. The key is to get the pH right (5.5 to 7.0). Most forest compost has a pH of 5.2 to 5.5, while peat moss has a pH of 4.0 to 5.5, depending upon the source. When perlite and lime are added to peat moss or forest compost, the outcome is a basic soilless mix.

Salvaged medium Preparation

Here is a formula to raise the pH and prepare a quality mix using forest compost or peat moss.

1. A 20-gallon garbage can (like the cheap Rubbermaid) is filled two-thirds full with rich, black forest compost or peat moss.

2. Perlite is added to the top and mixed thoroughly. The contents can be emptied and mixed on the ground with a pitchfork or gloves. A grower should wear a respirator or good dust mask for all mixing. A cement mixer is another option.

3. 5 to 6 cups of fine dolomite lime (with or without ¾ to 1 cup of hydrated lime) is added and thoroughly mixed in.

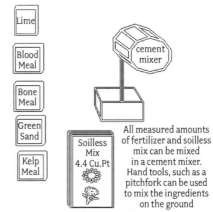

Figure 4.310: Mix materials.

A grower can make homemade mixes before adding the fertilizers to the home-made soilless mix. Mix recipes are described on pages 167 to 174.

Forest compost comes from a mature forest. It exists in a mature forest under a layer of sticks and needles. It is located a few inches beneath the needle layer. Some stores sell forest compost mixtures. It is usually free of stones, has a pH greater than 5, and should contain beneficial mycorrhizae. All loose roots should be removed from forest compost before it is used.

Peat moss comes from peat bogs. Peat bogs exist in areas of poor drainage that stay wet all year long.

Organic Fertilizing Recipes for Soilless Mix / Forest Compost / Peat Moss

Note: quarts and liters are about equal, and 4 quarts = approximately 1-gallon.

A. 1. Four 3.8 to 4 cubic foot bales of Sunshine #2 Mix, Jiffy Mix, Pro Mix, or other soilless mix.

2. Four bags of composted steer manure (20 to 30 quarts each bag).

3. One gallon of blood meal.

4. One gallon of steamed bonemeal.

5. One gallon of greensand.

6. Two quarts of kelp meal.

7. 0 to 50 quarts of perlite and / or 0 to 50 quarts of vermiculite.

8. Up to ⅓ parts soil.

Note: mix without soil is classed as organic hydroponic.

B. 1. One 3.8 to 4.0 cubic foot bale of Sunshine #2 Mix, Jiffy Mix, Pro Mix, or other soilless mix.

2. One 10kg bag of Welcome Harvest Farm Flower Power.

3. ½ to 1 bag of composted steer manure (10 to 30 quarts).

4. One quart of alfalfa meal.

5. 0 to 40 quarts of perlite.

6. Up to ⅓ parts soil.

C. 1. One 3.8 to 4.0 cubic foot bale of Sunshine #2 Mix, Jiffy Mix, or Pro Mix.

2. 5kg of Welcome Harvest Farm Flower Power.

3. One 20 to 30 quart bag of composted steer manure.

4. Eight cups of canola meal.

5. Three cups of blood meal.

6. One quart of greensand.

7. Perlite and vermiculite, as desired.

8. Up to ⅓ parts soil.

D. 1. One 3.8 to 4.0 cubic foot bale of Sunshine #2 Mix, Jiffy Mix, or Pro Mix.

2. ½ bag (10 to 15 quarts) of chicken manure.

3. ½ bag (10 to 15 quarts) of composted steer manure.

4. Four cups of blood meal.

5. Four cups of kelp meal.

6. Four cups of greensand.

7. Four cups of steamed bonemeal (pellet form).

8. 0 to 4 quarts (liters) well-decomposed compost.

9. 0 to 50 quarts of any combination of perlite and vermiculite

10. Up to ⅓ parts soil.

E. 1. One 3.8 to 4.0 cubic foot bale of Sunshine #2 Mix, Jiffy Mix, Pro Mix, or other soilless mix.

2. One bag of mushroom manure (20 to 30 quarts).

3. Two cups of langbeinite.

4. Four cups of greensand.

5. Four cups of kelp meal.

6. One quart of blood meal.

Plants got lots of light which helped produce larger buds from top to bottom.

7. One quart of steamed bonemeal.

8. 2.2kg of Welcome Harvest Farm Flower Power.

9. 0 to 30 quarts of vermiculite and / or perlite.

10. Up to ⅓ parts soil.

F.   1. One 3.8 to 4.0 cubic foot bale of Sunshine #2 Mix, Jiffy Mix, Pro Mix, or other soilless mix.

2. 9kg (20lbs) of pure earthworm castings (beware of imitators).

3. One 20 to 30 quart bag of composted steer manure.

4. One 5kg bag of Welcome Harvest Farm Flower Power.

5. Perlite/vermiculite combination, as desired.

6. Up to ⅓ parts soil.

G.   1. One 3.8 to 4.0 cubic foot bale of Sunshine #2 Mix, Jiffy Mix, Pro Mix, or other soilless mix.

2. 9kg (20lbs) of pure earthworm castings.

3. One 20 to 30 quart bag of composted steer manure.

4. One quart of blood meal.

5. Two quarts of steamed bonemeal.

6. One quart of kelp meal.

7. One quart of greensand.

8. 0 to 50 quarts or any perlite / vermiculite combination.

9. Up to ⅓ parts soil.

H.   1. One 3.8 to 4.0 cubic foot bale of Sunshine #2 Mix, Jiffy Mix, Pro Mix, or other soilless mix.

2. 9kg (20lbs) of pure earthworm castings.

3. 20 quarts of well-decomposed compost.

4. One quart of bonemeal.

5. One quart of greensand.

6. 0 to 50 quarts of any perlite / vermiculite combination.

7. Up to ⅓ parts soil.

Why Use Soilless Mix?

Soilless mix is made from organic peat, which holds nutrients, moisture, and air very effectively. It is versatile for all climates, and the grower has complete control over the fertilizing of the grow medium. Also, it is pH buffered which allows pH control. To put it simply, it allows the grower to get high end results with minimal effort.

Calcium peroxide, available under many trade names, can be added to any mixture. It breaks down into oxygen and lime and adds oxygen to the roots.

Other Organic Fertilizer Substitutes
Nitrogen

Some people don't like using blood meal, although it is one of the cheapest and strongest-acting dried nitrogen sources for the amount used. The numbers on the organic fertilizer packs do not represent the nitrogen of value to the plant, they represent the percentage of the fertilizer in the product. All organic nitrogen fertilizers release nitrogen at different rates. Other nitrogen sources are composted chicken manure, earthworm castings, fish meal, alfalfa meal, feather meal, and canola meal.

Phosphorous

Rock phosphate is a phosphorous additive. This can work well on its own or in combination with bonemeal. Bonemeal and rock phosphate release phosphorous for an entire growing season.

Potash

Kelp meal and greensand are good sources, and so is langbeinite. Crushed granite is good, too, but it should be the type that contains a decent supply of potassium feldspar. Greensand releases slowly and for more than a season. Nevertheless, a cup per plant each year is good to add. Kelp has a single-season limitation.

Trace minerals

There is no substitute for the many trace elements that kelp releases. However, many mined minerals work well too, such as greensand, Pyro Clay, and Mineral Magic.

Some liquid organic fertilizers, such as Earth Juice and Meta Naturals, have formulas that are made to contain trace elements.

Putting the Mix in the Proper Containers

Size is important. Larger containers allow for lower maintenance. Larger plants grow better in larger containers when plants are fertilized and watered periodically, such as when the mix begins to dry up. For a cycle of more than 3 months, it is recommended to use 1 to 3 gallons of mix per month of total growth before harvest.

Supplemental Fertilization/ Watering

The easiest method is to add a fertilizer application when the plants need a watering, then plain water can be used every second watering. The key to any fertilizing regime is not to overdo it, or to under do it. There are many water-soluble organic fertilizers on the market, such as Earth Juice and Meta Naturals.

Plants should never be starved of water to the point where they wilt. Wilting leaves is a sign of neglect. When plants stay wilted, some leaves will begin to dry up and die.

Chemical Cheat Sheet

Organic fertilizers work well on their own, but they can be used in conjunction with chemical fertilizers. Many growers use dried and water-soluble organic fertilizers throughout vegetative growth, then switch to chemical fertilizers during bloom.

Another approach is to use a synthetic blend of water-soluble chemical fertilizers during vegetative growth as well. Often, a single application of a cheap chemical fertilizer during vegetative growth will push a plant further than no application at all.

All formulas from chapter 4 will work, but here are some more that have done well for plants in vegetative growth or flowering.

Water-Soluble Fertilizers
Vegetative growth

During vegetative growth, applying one or more applications of a water-soluble chemical fertilizer, such as half to full-strength 20-20-20, will produce more vigorous growth. Adding Epsom salts (½-teaspoon per gallon) and the recommended rate of liquid kelp works well with a synthetic chemical blend.

The beauty of adding the odd chemical fertilizer application with the organic mix is that plants do not need these chemicals on a regular basis, since so many other sources of the nutrition are already available. And the odd shot of chemical fertilizer will not build up salts in the soil to the point where reusing the grow medium in the future will give deficient results.

Product quality will not be sacrificed if chemical and organic fertilizers reach a harmonic balance when used together.

Rooted clones growing in rockwool cubes which hold plenty of liquid nutrient between feedings.

Bloom

During bloom, one to three applications of a water-soluble chemical fertilizer such as GGold Nutrient Series, Miracle Grow 15-30-15, Plant Prod 15-30-15, General Hydroponics bloom, Dyna Bloom, etc., can be made. The dose can range anywhere from half to full strength. Epsom salts (added at ½-teaspoon per gallon) and the recommended rate of liquid kelp can be added to the chemical fertilizer, too. Fertilizers should not be added for the last two to three weeks of blooming, unless plants get a good flushing to remove salts in the growing medium no less than a week before harvesting.

Flushing Out Fertilizer

When procedures given in this manual are followed, the final product should be of top quality. However, flushing plants with lots of plain water two weeks before harvest and upwards until harvest can remove lots of salts. This flushing will improve the final product. In general, these formulas with organic mixes should work out fine without the need for flushing, unless many supplemental feedings are added. A major benefit of organic fertilizer usage is that salts are not a by-product of organic fertilizers, unlike chemical fertilizers, especially the cheap ones.

Nevertheless, adding a few doses of chemical fertilizer during cultivation can increase the volume without sacrifice to quality.

If flushing is necessary, using large amounts of plain water or using one of the many flushing formulas available in the market today is recommended. These flushing formulas attach to the fertilizer salts and unused elements in the growing medium, so that they will be removed. Some clearing solutions come in flavors like pina colada and strawberry. They will alter the smoke flavor.

Some flushing formulas should be followed up with a dose of plain water in order to remove an undesirable flavor that they leave behind.

Flushing formulas will come with instructions.

Reusing Soilless Mix/ Forest Compost

When the indoor crop is finished, the mix can be reused, meaning that the grow medium can be used over and over again. This is beneficial: after each crop is done, the grow mix retains its investment value, since it can be reused indefinitely. The chart shows how mix volume increased year in, year out. Only new fertilizers need to be added for each additional grow.

Method

A. All roots must be pulled out of the mix.

B. Tap water can be used to flush salts out of the medium, if chemical fertilizer was applied in excess. If fertilizer was not applied in excess, the grow medium only needs to be sterilized as described below.

C. A PPM meter is used to measure the PPM of the runoff solution. When the runoff is near the same PPM as the tap water, the salts are gone from the mix.

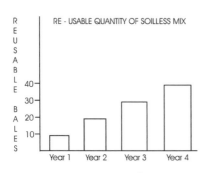

Figure 4.311: Mix retains value.

D. ½ to 1 tablespoon of calcium peroxide per gallon of mix can be added to the reused mix to help sterilize it.

Adding 35% hydrogen peroxide at a rate of 2ml per gallon of water during watering can help sterilize the soilless mix, too. Giving the medium a good soaking before transplanting is a cheap and easy way to sterilize it.

Soilless Mix V-System

Introduction

This system is used to grow small plants that will produce nice top buds, growing in 1-gallon pots. They are spaced at 8 to 10-inch centers. This system is more productive than a Sea of Green flat garden because a grower can cultivate more plants per square foot. It can be constructed with 2x4 wood, 1x6 wood, and nails for less than $30.

Materials

1. Six 12-foot lengths of 2x4 wood.
2. Four 12-foot lengths of 1x6 wood.
3. 3½-inch nails.

Figure 4.312: Simple V-system using pots and plant dishes.

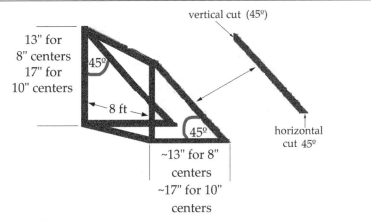

Figure 4.313 : Building the support system.

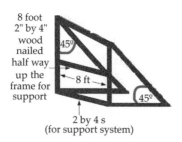

8 foot
2" by 4"
wood
nailed
half way
up the
frame for
support

←— 8 ft —→

45°

45°

2 by 4 s
(for support system)

Figure 4.314: Adding support.

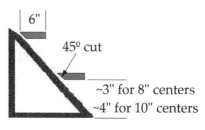

| 6" |

45° cut

~3" for 8" centers
~4" for 10" centers

Figure 4.315: Shelf for pots.

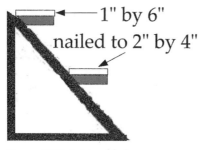

←— 1" by 6"

nailed to 2" by 4"

Figure 4.316: 1x6 is added.

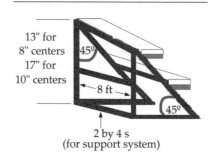

13" for
8" centers
17" for
10" centers

45°

←— 8 ft —→

45°

2 by 4 s
(for support system)

Figure 4.317: Completed platform.

Tools

1. Hammer.

2. Handsaw or circular saw.

3. Measuring tape.

Setup

A. The 2x4s are nailed together to make two right-angled triangles. The bottom width is 13 inches long and the height is 13 inches if the plants are spaced 8 inches apart. (Figure 4.313) Two frames are used in the system. (Figure 4.312)

B. The right-angled triangles are nailed together with two 2x4s. A small system could be 4 feet long, a longer system 7 to 8 feet long. (Figure 4.314)

A 2x4 is used to connect the two vertical pieces of 2x4 to give additional support. (Figure 4.314)

C. Two 6-inch pieces of 2x4 are nailed to the front of the frame 3 inches and 6 inches from the bottom. The 2x4 has 45° cuts next to the frame so that the top of it lies flat. (Figure 4.315)

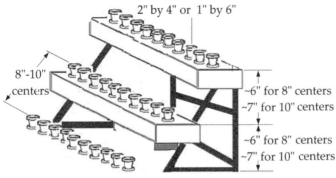

Figure 4.318: Spacing is critical to get a concentrated yield in a given space.

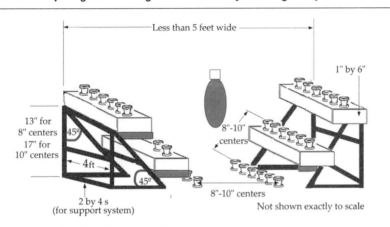

Figure 4.319: 4-foot by 5-foot setup picture A

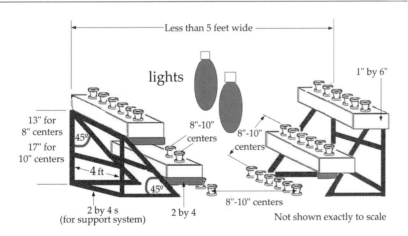

Figure 4.320: 4-foot by 5-foot setup picture B

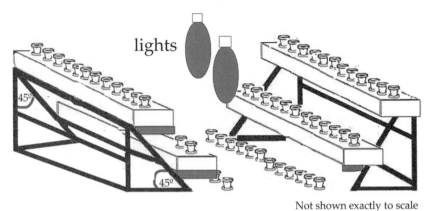

Not shown exactly to scale

Figure 4.321: 8-foot by 5-foot setup picture A

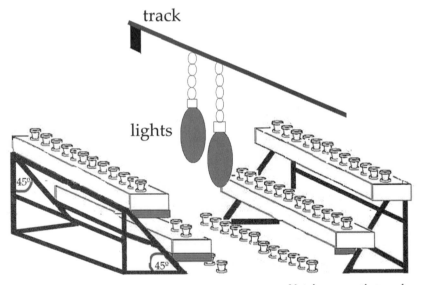

Not shown exactly to scale

Figure 4.322: 8-foot by 5-foot setup picture B

D. A 1x6 is nailed on top of the 2x4. (Figure 4.316)

E. 1-gallon pots with soilless mix are placed 8 inches apart on three different levels. 5 to 6 plants can be used for a 4-foot system, and 9 to 12 plants for an 8-foot system. (Figures 4.317 and 4.318) Plant dishes can be placed under each pot, or a plastic sheet can be placed on the floor to keep it clean.

Soil Growing

Introduction

This section covers growing with soil, although it is not the recommended method. To get to the point: soil belongs outside. Growers that fear hydroponic mediums should perhaps try using soilless mix, which looks and feels like dirt. Soilless mix is sterile and contains no nutrients. Soilless mix is easier to control. Here are a few reasons why soil should be left where it comes from:

1. The growth rate could be as low as half that of plants grown in a hydroponic system.

2. It is more work to move and prepare heavy soil from the outdoors while hydroponic mediums are dry and lightweight, and aeroponics uses air that needs no transporting.

3. It is harder to flush fertilizers out of soil than out of a hydroponic medium because in most cases, soil drains poorly.

4. Fertilizer costs will be higher.

5. Yield potential is higher with hydroponics / aeroponics.

A. Finding and Preparing Quality Dirt

Quality topsoil can be purchased at a decent price. Quality dirt can also be found in quality outdoor garden topsoil, in mature forests (forest compost), under deciduous tree canopies (composted organic matter) such as alder trees, and at creek beds.

Soil tests can be made with inexpensive soil test kits available at garden centers. If tests are made, it is recommended that you keep a log in order to reference how well a technique works in specific dirt.

B. pH Test

A grower can get the pH tested at a garden center for a couple of bucks, or a pH test kit or pH meter can be used to measure the pH. If this is done at a garden center, they will give you exact instructions regarding how to bring the pH up to the desired 6.5 to 7.0 range. For a grower that wants to do his own pH testing, cheap test kits are available from garden centers.

Dolomite lime has a neutral pH and makes adjusting the pH to 7.0 a piece of cake. Adding lime early is important to neutralize the pH, so that calcium and other elements can be utilized later during the grow season. It takes a few months for dolomite to break down and become available to the plants.

C. Adding Material to Improve the Soil

Sand, perlite, peat moss, or vermiculite can now be added and evenly mixed to loosen and aerate the soil. Perlite will allow water to drain well and is therefore beneficial for a wetter soil. Vermiculite will hold water and is good for a drier soil. Sand will help heat the soil and is good for slow-draining soil type, as it loosens up the dirt and allows for decent drainage. Peat holds water, air, and nutrients. Adding ⅓ of any of these amendments is a good idea. Adding ⅓ peat and ⅓ perlite works, too.

D. Adding Fertilizer

A soil test is made with a soil test kit, or can be obtained from a garden center, to determine levels of nitrogen, phosphorous, and potassium. However, for each plant, 1 cup of blood meal, 1 to 2 cups of bonemeal, 1 cup of greensand, and 1 cup of kelp meal can be added to any size container from 2 to 20 gallons for the purpose of a backup food supply. More plant food can be added later to give a plant required nutrients. Any recommended rate of a commercial fertilizer designed for "flowering plants" applied at half of full strength will work fine during vegetative growth and flowering. Alternating a watering with plain water and a watering with fertilizer will yield half-decent results.

5

Maintaining the Grow Room

In this chapter, the instructions for building common simple and sophisticated growing systems have been detailed.

The next chapter will explain how simple it is to give the plants close to ideal growing conditions through climate control and the use of commercial and homemade plant food formulas. The idea is to give the plants what they need to reach near their maximum yield and quality potential.

To make the most of an indoor grow room, a grower must maintain the room. The following variables, 1 to 14, are discussed in this chapter. The variables for routine maintenance are:

1. Parts per million (the fertilizer concentration)
2. Solution PH (the acidity or alkalinity level)
3. Understanding the Hydroponic medium
4. The Feeding formula
5. Organic Hydroponics
6. Water quality
7. Carbon Dioxide
8. Lighting
9. Temperature and humidity
10. High-tech climate control
11. Power Consumption
12. Foliar Feeding

These plants have had proper routine maintenance.

13. Predators

14. Pruning and Bending

This chapter explains the above variables in detail. The previous chapter described a number of systems for building a grow room, which, if properly carried out, will help control some of these variables, such as good air flow.

Calculating Parts Per Million

A chemical nutrient solution should be at 1,000 to 1,500PPM (parts per million) to be on the safe side in most cases, but custom adjustments (i.e. 800PPM) can be made depending upon the plant and stage of growth. Hydroponic systems that do not recirculate solutions make it much easier to produce precise nutrient levels. A basic TDS meter (which tests for total dissolved solids) will give a reading in PPM, such as 1,200. Expensive meters measure a large span of elements and can be used to keep all feeding costs to the bare minimum because specific nutrients can be added after they are used by the plants.

An organic or a chemical-organic fertilized nutrient solution should be no higher than 1,500PPM. With an organic or a chemical-organic solution, a grower can push the quantity of certain elements in a solution because a lot of the

A poor diet or sketchy growing conditions can leave nasty results.

fertilizer will not contain salts that hinder growth when they are in a solution in excess. For example, when Earth Juice Grow and Earth Juice Bloom are used to obtain the desired PPM of nitrogen and calcium, the PPM on a meter would be lower than if a solution of calcium nitrate was used to give the same PPM of nitrogen and calcium.

There will be dissolved solids in an organic hydroponic system from sources such as bat guano, Epsom salts (magnesium sulphate), sulphate of potash, humic acid, etc. Some fertilizers will add nutrients, but the PPM meter will not fluctuate. In a nutshell, this is the advantage of many organic fertilizers: they deposit no toxic salts. Results will be excellent if an organic solution is changed weekly, every ten days, or every second week with a good fertilizing formula. A solution can go unchanged for longer periods of time with additions of new nutrients from time to time, especially when plants are small and don't feed as much. However, since plant nutrient requirements are always changing and some nutrient deficiencies are hard to detect, it is advised that you change the solution regularly to avoid the hassle of determining what plant food is needed and when. Also, just because plants are green doesn't mean that they are growing at maximum production rate.

Monitoring the Reservoir
Drain to Waste Hydroponic Systems

A system that does not recirculate the nutrient solution is easy to use because the same formula can be made each time the plants get fed. In most systems, 2 quarts (liters) or less per plant is enough of a solution to feed each plant.

Recirculating Hydroponic Systems

Plants in a recirculating hydroponic system that uses a pump need more monitoring because pH and PPM will change.

What Size Reservoir?

A major factor worth noting is that larger reservoirs will have less fluctuations in PPM and pH and will minimize maintenance.

Using 5 to 12 gallons of solution is fine for small or large closets during vegetative growth and flowering.

Using 20 to 40 gallons of solution would be fine in a bedroom. For example, 20 gallons of solution for vegetative growth would require little maintenance. During flowering, 40 gallons of solution is low maintenance.

Young Plants

Young plants tend to use more water than nutrient. Therefore, for the first 2 to 4 weeks, adding plain water to the reservoir is probably all that is necessary because solution will become saline(i.e. 1,800PPM) when a plant takes in water without much nutrient. Until plants start to use a decent amount of nutrient, it is not necessary to do complete reservoir changes, because there will be nutrients that have not yet been used by the plants. 600 to 1,000PPM is adequate for seedlings and vegetative growth.

Aging Plants

It doesn't hurt to make a solution on the weak side (i.e. 1,000 PPM) until plants start to use equal parts nutrient and water, because PPM will rise as water is used by the plants.

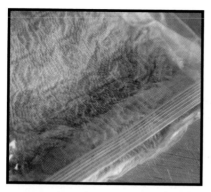

To start the germination process, seeds are wrapped in a moist towel inside a ziplock bag.

After a couple of days of moisture, the seeds can be given a germination check.

Seeds can be checked daily to see if new growth had started.

A white tail emerges from a moist seed.

The new growth takes off fast after it emerges from the seed.

Seedlings should be transplanted before they are ½-inch long.

New shoots on a healthy growing clone can look a little yellow before they green up.

The first sign of the plant's sex can be seen above the intersection at the plant nodes and the main stalk.

Crowded seedlings that are not stunted can be spooned out and transplanted.

Cutting in rockwool cube.

Rubber gloves can be worn for extra sanitary precautions.

Rockwool cubes can be cut to accommodate a transplant.

Small rooting cube transplanted into a larger rockwool cube.

Cuttings root in a common nursery flat that is available at most garden shops.

Clones have been transplanted into rockwool cubes that are placed on expanded clay pellets.

The roots will eventually spread out like a carpet at the bottom of the clay.

Commercial aeroponic cloning chambers allow the cuttings to form roots very quickly, in as few as 5 to 7 days.

Oscillating fan moves the air around.

Flooding and draining is the technique used to feed this crop.

Lightly pressing around the pot can make the plant come out easily for transplanting.

Using a solution that has a known ph is used to test and calibrate a ph meter.

Rooms must be clean and clothes should be lint-free because fabrics can easily snag on the bud hairs.

Cheap 2x2s can be used to support and train plants for maximum light usage.

Plants get tied to a support system to allow for a greater yield.

Maturing bud will soon have pistils that will change color and die.

Buds that look fine still need flushing in order to taste good.

Crispy, skinny buds can be cased by heat, shock, or insufficient darkness.

Close up of a nug.

The top bud is always the biggest on the limb.

Buds are removed so that no stalk is present.

Overhead view of the top bud.

Small leaves and lumber (stalks) that do not get picked are a sign of sloppy manicuring and they do not add any significant weight.

Small buds can be graded and placed in a separate bag.

The waste stalks make good kindling.

Manicured buds are drying on the stalks.

String is hung on hooks to support dehydrating buds.

String is tied in tiers so that these buds can be dried in a small space.

Gardens must be enclosed so that no light gets in during the dark hours.

Netting is a great way to position budding marijuana plants.

Wall to wall bud is the grower's ideal.

Laying 6-ml black plastic on the floor is a cheap method of avoiding spills and keeping a carpet clean.

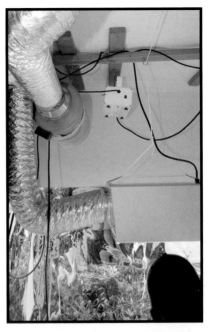

Air-cooled hoods allow more light to be used in a room.

Airy buds with more leaf will always look inferior to tight nugs with less leaf.

Mold can start from the inner nodes and work its way outside.

Timers run various lamps and other equipment during the specified hours.

Enough plants to cover the room, but without crowding.

Leaf overlap will diminish light access for the lower leaves.

Many manufacturers make high quality bulbs for indoor horticulture.

Sodium lights are narrow and long.

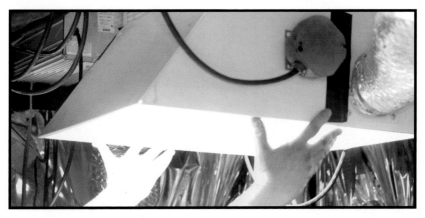

Air-cooled hoods provide less intense heat to the plants, especially those directly under the light.

Buds are hung on a line to dry.

These plants have been given enough room to dry evenly.

The endless leaves on these buds will make the picking process practically Sisyphean.

Squashing your buds, although tempting, is not wise.

Nutrients are recirculated in this top feeding hydroponic system.

When plants use equal parts nutrient and water, adding 1,000 to 1,500 PPM concentrated solution is recommended.

When plants use more nutrient than water, adding a concentrated solution of about 1,500PPM is recommended, unless a stronger concentration is needed to keep PPM at optimal levels. One should try to keep the PPM near 1,500PPM in the reservoir. This way the solution will stay within the 1,000 to 1,500PPM boundaries, even as PPM slowly drops as plants use more nutrient than water.

Green leaves and the absence of leaf curl from top to bottom of the plant are signs that the plant is getting adequate nutrition.

When a reservoir needs changing (i.e. every 1 to 2 weeks), it is a good idea to allow the solution to run low. For example, if a full reservoir is at 1,500PPM, it is possible to allow water and nutrient to lower to a level such as 800PPM. This will give a little flush since the solution is on the weak side. Now there is only a little liquid to pump out of the reservoir before a new solution is added, thus minimizing maintenance.

Plants that are close to intense light will use nutrient up more quickly than plants that receive less intense light.

When plants do not get the correct doses of food, nutrient deficiencies occur. When a deficiency occurs, leaves normally change color from green to green-yellow to yellow. Deficiencies are often a sign that the reservoir needs a change, or specific elements need to be added to the reservoir.

When a deficiency occurs, it is recommended that you give the plants the food they crave (i.e. nitrogen or calcium). Nitrogen is the most common deficiency.

Deficiencies should change within a day or two after the proper fertilizer is applied, and plant should go back to a healthy green unless the deficiency caused serious damage.

How to Use and Clean a TDS Meter

A. The TDS meter electrodes should be rinsed with clean or distilled water,

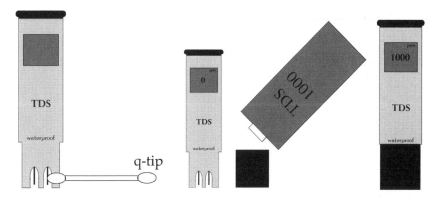

Figure 5.1: The probes are scrubbed with a q-tip.

Figure 5.2: Calibrating solution is placed into the cap or a tiny cup.

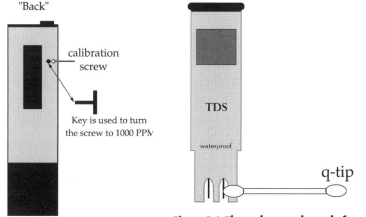

Figure 5.3: Adjusting the meter reading.

Figure 5.4: The probes are cleaned after each use.

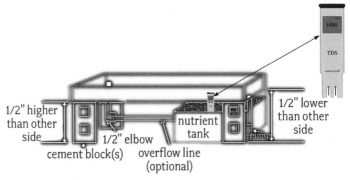

1/2" higher than other side

cement block(s)

1/2" elbow

nutrient tank

overflow line (optional)

pump

1/2" lower than other side

TDS

Figure 5.5: Checking the PPM in the nutrient tank.

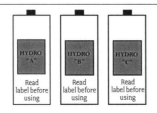

Figure 5.6: Three part hydroponic formula.

or isopropyl alcohol, then water. A Q-tip helps scrub the electrodes free of debris too.

B. Now the meter should be submersed in a calibrating solution (1,000PPM). A small container or the protective cap around the electrodes serves as a place to hold the calibrating solution.

C. The calibration dial should be turned until the reading shows that of the calibrating solution (i.e. 1,000PPM). (Figure 5.5) Some meters come with a calibration screwdriver while others need a small screwdriver.

D. The electrodes should be cleaned again with a Q-tip and clean water.

E. The meter should be dipped in the reservoir after the fertilizer is added.

F. Fertilizer or water should be added to adjust the PPM reading to between 1,000 to 1,500PPM.

If the PPM is higher than wanted, adding water can dilute the solution to the desired PPM range. The meter is actually useless in determining proper amounts of an organic or chemical-organic solution, but it is a good reference meter. Further in this chapter we will discuss organic formulations, chemical formulations, and how to get the desired PPM of a specific element (e.g. nitrogen) in a fertilizer.

Hopefully your water source is near 0 PPM so that water is not stocked with unwanted PPM, which can put limits on the amount of fertilizer that may be added to a solution. There are many relatively inexpensive products, such as reverse osmosis machines and distillation devices, which remove unwanted dissolved solids from a water supply.

Note: The PPM readings should only be used as a reference for changing solutions because they do not read the actual parts per million of a solution. Calculating parts per million of a particular fertilizer or element is best done with a little math and chemistry calculation as will be explained on the next page.

Most meters are priced under $100. These measure PPM on a scale of 100 (i.e. 100, 500, 1,000, 1,100). For most people, these meters do the deed. However, there are expensive meters that measure a wide variety of elements in a solution. These tools are for experienced hydroponic farmers.

Determining PPM without a Meter

The percentage of the element in a fertilizer (i.e. 20-20-20) is needed to determine the PPM.

The fertilizer packs are listed as NPK. N is all nitrogen, but phosphorous is listed as a compund (P_2O_5), and potassium (K) is listed as K_2O.

Phosphorous(P) is 44% of phosphoric acid (P_2O_5), potassium(K) is 83% of Potash (K_2O).

To get the PPM from a 15-30-15 fertilizer, the first step is to take all three numbers and move the decimal one place to the right. In the case of nitrogen, the number would be 150. This number will give the parts per million of nitrogen when 1-gram is added to each quart or liter.

For phosphorous, a grower should multiply the 300 by .44. For example, 300 x .44 = 142PPM. This number will give the parts per million of phosphorous when 1-gram is added to each quart or liter.

For potassium, a grower should multiply the 150 by .83. For example, 150 x .83 = 124.5 PPM. This number will give the parts per million of potassium when 1-gram is added to each quart.

Advanced Note: Some growers make their own plant food with 5 to 7 basic salts, like those described on pages 196 to 199.

How to Get the Percentage of an Element (i.e. K=potassium) in a Compound (i.e. K₂SO₄)

Here is how to get desired parts per million of sulphur(S) and potassium (K) in potassium sulphate (K_2SO_4).

A. The periodic table of elements should be referenced in order to get the atomic numbers of each atom. For example, potassium has an atomic number of 19, sulphur has an atomic number of 16, and oxygen has an atomic number of 8.

B. Now, to determine the percentage of each element, all the elements must have their atomic numbers multiplied by the number of ions in a compound. In the case of K_2SO_4, the atomic number of potassium, (K), which is 19, is multiplied by 2 to give 38, because there are 2 potassium ions. Since there is only one sulphur ion, 16 is multiplied by 1 to give 16. Oxygen has four ions in the compound, therefore 8 is multiplied by 4 to give 32.

C. Now all of the atomic numbers are multiplied by the number of ions, and all of the atoms multiplied by their atomic weights are added up. For example, the total number in potassium sulphate is (2 x 19) + 16 + (4 x 8) = 86.

D. To get the percentage of each element, the amount of ions is multiplied by the element's atomic number. For example, in the case of potassium, 2 x 19 = 38.

E. The amount of ions multiplied by the element's atomic number is divided by the sum of all the elements multiplied by their atomic numbers. In the case of potassium, the 38 (number of ions x atomic number) is divided by 86 (which equals .44).

F. The number multiplied by 100 gives the percentage. For potassium, .44 x 100 = 44%.

G. Finally, the percentage number should have the decimal place moved over one place to the right. In the case of potassium, the number would be 440. This number will give the parts per million of an element when 1-gram is added to each quart or liter. In the potassium case, 1-gram of potassium in a quart of liquid will give 440PPM of potassium. Using half a gram per quart will give 220PPM of potassium and 95 parts per million of sulphur.

Available PPM

The level of solubility (and purity) in water will make the final say. For example, some solutions and powders will completely dissolve into usable ions, while others will not be soluble in water, hence the elements will not be readily available to plants. For example, gypsum ($CaSO_4$) is not very soluble in water, which makes it almost useless for hydroponics. However, gypsum does break down slowly in soil, where it works fine. All formulas in this chapter are nearly 100% soluble in water.

How to pH a Solution

The pH level is the measure of the hydrogen ion concentration in a solution or other medium. There are more hydrogen ions in an acid solution than in a basic solution. On a scale, a pH of 7.0 is neutral, under 7.0 is acidic, and over 7.0 is alkaline. A plant's intake of certain elements is greatly affected by pH.

A. The pH of plain water should be checked before adding the fertilizers. That pH number should be written down where it can easily be found. If the water pH is the same in the future, it is easier to make a quick formula using the same fertilizers without having to measure.

B. All of the fertilizers can be added and mixed well. The quantities should be written down for future reference.

C. A clean pH pen should be calibrated at 7.0, which is the pH reading of the calibrating solution. Calibration instructions are given on page 193.

D. The pen should be dipped into the solution and pH up or pH down should be added until the reading is in the 5.5 to 6.5 range. In many cases using chemical fertilizers, the ph will drift down. Therefore, making the ph at a higher number like 6.5 will allow the PH to be in the desired range until it drifts downward.

E. The electrodes should be rinsed in clean water before the meter is put away.

An example of a pH up product is Greenfire Natural Up. There are endless pH up solutions available anywhere garden supplies are available. Using feeding

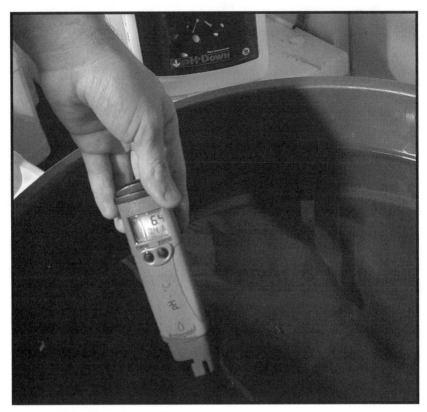

The pH of the solution is checked.

combinations that don't rock the pH level means little or no pH up is needed.

An example of organic pH down is Earth Juice Natural Down. Vinegar also works fine. There are many brands of ph down available.

Writing down the quantity of pH up or pH down that is added (for future reference) is a good method for putting together an identical solution in the future.

pH Drift

The pH should be checked daily and adjusted if necessary because many fertilized solutions will drift significantly upward or downward in pH in less than 24 hours. Organic fertilizers tend to drift upward in pH after being mixed, and may continue to do so for a day or up to a few days after the solution is mixed. Adding molasses and avoiding certain fertilizers can keep the upward pH drift in a solution (organic or chemical-organic) to a minimum.

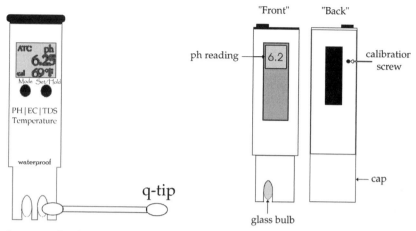

Figure 5.7: The glass bulbs are cleaned.　　**Figure 5.8: The typical pH meter.**

Making an organic (or chemical-organic) solution a day or two in advance, with molasses (1½ml / gallon of water) helps against upward pH drift.

How to Clean the pH Pen
If a pH pen is not cleaned after each day it is used, it can be hard to get accurate readings and it may not calibrate to the correct reading, especially if organic fertilizers are used. Using a cleaning solution on it before putting it away helps calibrate the pen accurately. The pen should be allowed to stay moist when it is put away. A few drops of calibrating solution in the bottom cap helps the electrodes stay moist. Cleaning the pH pen with clean tap water and a Q-tip works too, and saves money. When a Q-tip is used, it is recommended that you gently pull the fluff away from the stick so that the soft cotton batting can be moved between tough spaces. Care should always be taken for the glass, because it can break and start to give weird readings without a grower noticing the error.

How to Calibrate the pH Pen
A. After the pen is rinsed with plain water, a pH buffer 7.0 solution or distilled water is used to calibrate the pen. The solution can be placed in the pH pen's cap, or a small container. (Figure 5.8)

B. The meter should be adjusted by turning a calibration screw so that it reads 7.0. (Figure 5.8) It might need several seconds to reach a stable reading.

C. A cheap bottle of pH 4.0 can be used once in a while to determine the condition of the pH meter, to see that the pen calibrates at two different numbers, 4.0 and 7.0. Calibrating at 4.0 involves the same procedure as calibrating at 7.0. (Figure 5.8)

D. After the pH pen is calibrated, it should be rinsed well with clean water before a reading is taken, and after every reading. In fact, an eye should be kept on the pH of the water that is being used to rinse the pH pen. If the water is good, clean running, cold tap water, the pen will often stay at one number when it is rinsed.

Calibration Notes

If the pH pen is really clean and calibrated properly, it should stay calibrated for several readings. When the calibration does read differently it is probably because the pen needs a cleaning.

If the meter is not clean and it is calibrated, all readings can be inaccurate. Weak batteries can throw off the readings and make the pH pen function at a slower speed.

Hydroponic Mediums
Choosing a Hydroponic Medium

Choosing the proper hydroponic medium is the most important factor for a successful hydroponic garden. All mediums react to a fertilizing program differently, and the cost of mediums varies dramatically. Some local materials (i.e. fir bark, wood chips, small stones, and coconut fibers) are available for a cheap price. Most large-scale hydroponic farms use large quantities of local materials to keep the costs down, but a hobbyist may get better yields from commercial products such as clay, rockwool, or sterilized soilless mix that are cheap and convenient for smaller gardens.

For any medium, it is safe to feed for 5 to 6 days, then flush for 1 day with plain water (or a low PPM solution of, say, 400PPM). Some growers add 1 to 2ml of hydrogen peroxide / gallon of plain water during flushing to disinfect the system. A grower can flush throughout a plant's life cycle until within two weeks of harvest. Two weeks prior to harvest, growers often flush out the medium with a low PPM solution to get maximum flavor.

Preparing Mediums

Perlite compacts and should stand in a container of water for about a half hour. Fine particles of perlite will sink to the bottom of the water. The floating perlite is useful; what goes to the bottom of the barrel can go into compost or garden. Perlite is a good medium, but it does not cling on to elements. Therefore, plants must be well fed.

Clay floats, and should be soaked or sprayed until the water running through it becomes clear. Rinsing clay is similar to washing rice until the water runs clear. Clay is negatively charged and attracts positive ions such as calcium and potassium. Soaking rocklike mediums such as clay in water and 35% hydrogen peroxide (i.e. 2 to 5 ml / gallon of water) helps to sterilize the medium from any potential diseases. Sun heat helps sterilize mediums, too.

Careful Alert

Perlite and other mediums can clog the feeding system and keep it from allowing the solution to pump in, or to drain. All screens and filters may need a periodic cleaning and the pump should have panty hose (if used) cleaned during a reservoir change.

Reusing Mediums

All mediums (except disposable mediums like rockwool) can be reused if all roots are removed from the medium, and medium is sterilized between crops.

Clay pellets are cleaned with water or sterilized with hydrogen peroxide before they are used.

For example, clay, soilless mix, and round stones can be used indefinitely. Mediums can safely be sterilized with an application of 35% hydrogen peroxide (2 to 5 ml / gallon of water). Most mediums such as perlite can be composted or used immediately to improve soil. For example, broken down wood chips can go into compost, while perlite and soilless mix can go directly into the garden.

Mediums should be cleaned as soon as a crop is completed to avoid molds. Molds often build up while a moist medium (such as clay) sits unused. If necessary, a citrus cleanser can be used to clean the medium so that all molds and waxy buildup are removed. After the citrus cleanser is applied, the medium should be rinsed with plain water to remove the soaplike bubbles. A little leftover cleanser in the medium will not harm the plants.

Reusing Soilless Mix

Soilless mix can be sterilized with calcium peroxide so that the medium can be reused to grow more crops.

When the indoor crop is finished, the mix can be reused. This is beneficial, because after each crop is done, the grow mix retains its investment value, since it can be reused indefinitely.

The mix can be flushed with water until the PPM runoff is near 0 PPM.

Hydroponic Feeding Formulas
Vegetative Growth

Most hydroponic formulas are purchased in 1 to 3 parts. They will work fine when used at the recommended rate. When powdered fertilizers are mixed, it is possible to save lots of money. Here are a few formulas using basic fertilizer salts.

1. Calcium nitrate: add 1½ grams per liter (quart) or 1½ teaspoons per gallon (dissolved in ½ to 1 liter of warm water before adding to reservoir).
2. Potassium phosphate: ⅓-gram per liter (quart) or ¼-teaspoon per gallon (dissolved in ½ to 1 liter of warm water before adding to reservoir).
3. Potassium sulphate: ⅓-gram per liter (quart) or ⅙-teaspoon per gallon (dissolved in ½ to 1 liter of warm water before adding to reservoir).
4. Magnesium sulphate: (Epsom salts): ¼ to ½-gram per liter (quart) or ¼-teaspoon per gallon (dissolved in ½ to 1 liter of warm water before adding to reservoir). Note: 2 to 4 can be dissolved together.

Seaweed is a great source of micronutrients.

5. Chelated trace elements: $\frac{1}{10}$-teaspoon per gallon = $\frac{1}{2}$-teaspoon per 5 gallons (dissolved separately in warm water). Kelp, or kelp and a mineral powder, can be used in place of chelated trace elements.

This solution mixture will be dumped into a reservoir and the concentration will read around 1,300PPM on a TDS meter. In most cases, the solution should always fall between 1,000PPM and 1,500 PPM, unless medium is being flushed

Quality feeding and quality bud go hand in hand.

with dilute solution (i.e. 800PPM) or with plain water (very briefly) to remove salts. The pH should be adjusted to fall between 6.0 and 6.6.

Option: Seaweed products, humic acid, and vitamin B-1 may be added in small quantities. The PPM should be no higher than 1,500 if other products are added.

Flowering

pH buffered fertilizers are very user friendly. However, the dirt cheap formulas below are much cheaper to make using basic fertilizer salts. Like traditional hydroponic farmers, making homemade plant food is the major way to save money after a grow room is up and running.

1. Calcium nitrate: add 1-gram per liter (quart) or 1-teaspoon per gallon (dissolved in ½ to 1 liter of warm water before adding to reservoir). During late flowering, the calcium nitrate can be lowered to ½ to 1-gram per liter.

2. Potassium phosphate: ⅔-gram per liter (quart) or ½-teaspoon per gallon (dissolved in ½ to 1 liter of warm water before adding to reservoir).

3. Potassium sulphate: ⅕ to ¼-gram per liter (quart) or ⅛-teaspoon per gallon (dissolved in ½ to 1 liter of warm water before adding to reservoir).

4. Magnesium sulphate (Epsom salts): ¼ to ½-gram per liter (quart) or ¼-teaspoon per gallon (dissolved in ½ to 1 liter of warm water before adding to reservoir). Note: 2 to 4 can be dissolved together.

5. Chelated trace elements: ⅒-teaspoon per gallon or ½-teaspoon per 5 gallons (dissolved in ½ to 1 liter of warm water before adding to reservoir). Kelp, or kelp and a mineral powder can be used in place of chelated trace elements.

When a meter is used to read the PPM, it will read 1,300 PPM if the tap water had less than 100 PPM. If the tap water was something like 200 PPM, then the meter would read 1,500 PPM

The water pH should be adjusted to always lie between 5.5 and 6.3.

Some growers like to customize their formulas by adding products like liquid kelp, humic acid, and vitamin b-1.

Organic Hydroponics

The formulas in this section are designed for mediums that drain well such as perlite, coconut fibers, and clay pellets. These formulas will also work fine for soilless mix such as Sunshine Mix and Jiffy Mix. These have been formulated to give flowering plants all the necessary primary and secondary elements, as well as the trace elements necessary for vigorous growth. No salts will accumulate with the organic ingredients, thus providing a better tasting smoke with the end product. If quality is an issue and so is volume, the following sample formulas are definitely worth a try.

For complete control, cheap and light perlite is recommended for the medium because it does not alter the solution's pH and fertilizers do not cling to it. Perlite also allows lots of air to get in the spaces when solution drains through it. However, perlite needs regular irrigation, such as a few waterings a day, or continuous irrigation. Not for the sake of food necessity, but for the fact that dry perlite sends out a dust. This dust can collect on the top of leaves.

Clay is good medium, but it is heavy and a little expensive. It is negatively charged and will hold some positive ions such as calcium and potassium. All mediums can be flushed with plain water—or low PPM—regularly. For example, a grower can feed for 6 days and flush once a week during veg and flower.

Materials such as clay that alter the pH can be of use to keep the pH down. Also, holding some water and nutrients can be good too, especially between

One-gallon pump sprayers are good devices for foliar feeding, misting with plain water, and applying pesticides.

feedings when the water is drained from the growing medium.

Vegetative Growth

Any recommended rate from an organic fertilizer manufacturer should work fine. Feeding needs to be more precise during bloom. If chemicals are used during vegetative growth, and organics are used during bloom, nobody will be able to tell the difference from a garden grown only with organics. This is a way to make tasty produce on a skinny budget.

Vegetative Growth Formula A

Manufacturer's recommended rate for Sea Mix 3-2-2, or two-thirds of the recommended rate for Alaska Fish Fertilizer, combined with the recommended rate for liquid kelp. In addition, pH up or pH down can be added until the pH is between 6.0 and 6.5. Adding Epsom salts (magnesium sulphate), ½ to 1-teaspoon per 5 gallons will help combat magnesium and sulphur deficiencies.

Special note: All pH testing and addition of a pH up or pH down is optional, although recommended. Hydrogen peroxide usage at 1 to 3 ml / gallon is recommended to keep the medium clean.

Vegetative Growth Formula B

When it comes time for the second feeding, the fertilizing can be repeated. Here is an optional solution to use: Sea Mix, two-thirds of the manufacturer's recommended rate. Humic acid (made from organic molecules created from the breakdown of organic matter) at ⅕ to ⅔ of the recommended rate. Add pH up or pH down until the pH hits 6.0 to 6.5.

Vegetative Growth Formula C

Earth Juice or Meta Naturals products applied at the recommended rate.

Flowering

A grower can take any commercial fertilizer and mix it at the recommended rate and results will be fine, but in order to grow specific plants productively and with the lowest cost, making custom formulations is the way to go. All big-scale farms know the importance of making their own fertilizers, which is a major expense once the farm is set up.

After the grower can acquire the necessary components to make a custom blend, the next step is to mix a simple mixture.

During flowering, a grower cannot afford to be sloppy. Feeding is more critical and plants use more nutrients when they are producing flowers. Here are some sample formulas for this important stage of growth.

Bloom Formula A

1. Four teaspoons per gallon of Earth Juice Bloom.
2. Four teaspoons per gallon of Earth Juice Grow.
3. Four teaspoons of bat guano per gallon. Guano should be placed into a teabag or added directly into the tank. Bat guano can cause stomach aches when it is used in a recirculating hydroponic system, even with minimal exposure. For that reason, using the replacement (potassium phosphate) from the chemical cheat sheet (below) is safer than using bat guano. Or, more organically, using more Greenfire Earth Juice Bloom is another option.
4. Growth Plus (Nitrozyme) at ½-teaspoon per gallon
5. Epsom salts (magnesium sulphate) at ½ to 1-gram per quart (liter). Epsom salts should be dissolved in warm water, before adding to nutrient solution.

Budding plants growing in clay pellets.

6. One-gram per gallon of sulphate of potash (potassium sulphate) or 2 grams per quart (liter) of wood ashes. Sulphate of potash should be mixed separately in hot water for it to completely dissolve.

7. Finally, pH is adjusted to 5.5 to 6.5 with natural pH up or pH down.

Options: A grower can add the following to the above formula before adjusting PH.

1. Humic acid at 1-teaspoon per gallon or at ¼ to ⅓ the recommended rate.

2. For other trace minerals, a grower can add half to full recommended rate of liquid kelp.

3. Adding 1 tablespoon of molasses and 2 teaspoons of yeast into 1 quart (liter) is a cheap homemade catalyst. The mixture should be dissolved before it is added to the tank. It will add enzymes and help to combat upward pH drift.

The Bloom Formula solution should sit one or two nights so that pH stabilizes. Running a pump in the solution can help keep the solution agitated. Sometimes, some of the materials will flow to the bottom, such as bat guano, but most of this formula will stay nicely mixed. The pH of this solution will drift less upward the longer it sits in the nutrient tank. The pH should be monitored daily and adjusted to between 5.5 and 6.5, using either a natural pH up or a natural pH down.

Chemical Cheat Sheet

1. ½ to 1-gram of calcium nitrate can be used instead of Earth Juice Grow and Earth Juice Bloom.

2. A grower can use chelated trace minerals (½-teaspoon for every 5 gallons) while canceling the usage of Growth Plus (Nitrozyme) and Pyro Clay.

3. Using potassium phosphate at ½ to ¾-gram per quart (liter) allows a grower to eliminate the bat guano. The potassium levels can be changed during various stages of bloom to accommodate phosphorous levels.

Bloom Formula B

1. Four grams per quart (liter) of Pure Earthworm castings. Worm castings can be wrapped in panty hose, a teabag, or cheesecloth. Squeezing the castings in the bag periodically helps to release the fertilizer more quickly.

2. Four teaspoons per gallon of Earth Juice Bloom.

3. Four teaspoons of bat guano per gallon. Guano can be put in a teabag or panty hose. Guano should be squeezed periodically to release the fertilizer. (Warning: A formula with bat guano that is re-circulated may cause stomach aches.)

4. Growth Plus (Nitrozyme) at 1-teaspoon per gallon.

5. Epsom salts (magnesium sulphate) at ½ to 1-gram per quart (liter). Epsom salts should be dissolved in warm water before adding them to a nutrient solution.

6. One-gram per gallon of sulphate of potash (potassium sulphate) or 2 grams per quart (liter) of wood ashes. Sulphate of potash should be mixed

separately in hot water to completely dissolve the crystals before adding them to the nutrient solution.

The pH should be checked daily and adjusted to 5.5 to 6.5. A lower number is better for an upward drifting pH.

Options:

1. Pyro Clay can be added at 1-gram per liter.
2. Humic acid can be added at 1-teaspoon per gallon or at ¼ to ⅓ the recommended rate.
3. For other trace minerals, add half to full recommended rate of liquid kelp.
4. Adding 1 tablespoon of molasses and two teaspoons of yeast into 1 quart (liter) works as a catalyst. The mixture should be dissolved before it is added to the tank. The mixture will add enzymes and help combat upward pH drift.

Chemical Cheat Sheet

The first two substitutions must be made.

1. A grower may use ½ to 1-gram of calcium nitrate and the worm castings and Earth Juice Bloom can be eliminated from the original recipe.
2. Potassium phosphate at ½ to ¾-gram per quart (liter) can be added instead of bat guano. The potassium levels can be changed during various stages of bloom to accommodate phosphorous levels.
3. Using chelated trace minerals (½-teaspoon for every 5 gallons) can cancel the usage of Growth Plus (Nitrozyme) and Pyro Clay.

Special Notes—for All Organic Hydroponic Formulas

Solution should be topped up regularly (i.e. daily to weekly) with plain water or nutrient solution, depending on how the pH, PPM, and water level changes.

The pH of the solution should be checked and modified after adding liquid to the reservoir. Drawing a top-up line in the reservoir with a permanent felt-tip pen helps to make topping up the reservoir a brainless exercise. Large reservoirs that can run a few days to a week with proper pH and PPM make things even simpler.

The organic formulas I've given should be near 1,500PPM when read on a TDS meter after they have been mixed if the water supply reads at 0 PPM. A PPM meter can be used as a reference meter. A grower should take readings once in a

Rockwool cubes placed on top of clay pellets.

while to see if the PPM goes up or down.

Growers that make a large reservoir that contains all of the nutrients and holds a constant pH and PPM until the reservoir is changed have great results. This is not the most cost effective, but it is the easiest feeding method.

If the PPM stays the same or goes down just slightly, adding the regular solution that would be used normally can allow for minimal maintenance since the pH and PPM should be at desired levels. The grower may get lucky and find that he just needs to add some more new solution to the old solution to get great results without having to dump out the old batch. This is a money saving tip.

Making a solution that keeps a constant PPM (or only slightly lowering PPM) and is pH buffered gives the plants the exact elements they need until the reservoir becomes empty is the path to feeding perfection. This is perfect gardening if a grower can know exactly what to feed his plants when the solution runs low. This is expert territory.

If the PPM goes up, more water should be added to the tank to dilute the solution. With this approach, complete changes of solution are recommended, especially for larger plants that use up more nutrient than water.

Proper feeding will allow bud clusters to surround the stalks.

After a couple of weeks, an organic hydroponic solution can bring on odors, depending on the fertilizer (e.g. stinky bat guano).

If a PPM meter is used in an organic or chemical-organic garden, what works is changing the solution when the PPM drops to ⅓ to ½ of the original strength (i.e. PPM drops to 500 to 750 PPM). The waste can be poured out anywhere in an outdoor garden. Or additional amounts of the same formula can be added from time to time to replenish nutrients, if there is no smell. For the trained eye, individual nutrients can be added, such as Earth Juice Grow or bat guano, as deficiencies are spotted.

Nitrogen consumption is probably the heaviest of all the elements in the formulations. Changing the solution and replenishing all nutrients is the best move to keep things simple.

Water Quality
Purifying Water
Using pure, clean water is the easiest way to increase the yield in the garden.

The quality of an indoor water supply will vary from city to city, creek to creek, river to river, spring to spring, pond to pond, and well to well, not to mention rain water zones.

Water filters, reverse osmosis machines, distillation devices, and rainwater reservoirs are all methods of obtaining pure water. These purifying methods can be done for large and small quantities of water. Naturally, machines and filters

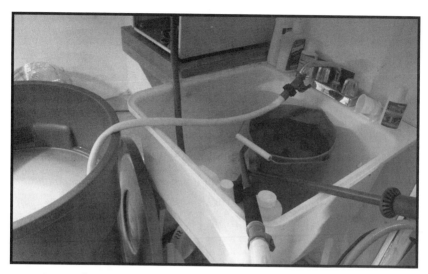

Water is poured into the reservoir.

that handle larger amounts of water will cost more.

Some machines and filters remove more dissolved solids than others. The better units normally cost more.

There are cheap filters that can be attached to faucets to remove chlorine from the water. Often, chlorine is the domestic gardener's worst enemy.

Desalinizing sea water is an expensive option for making quality use of sea water. Prices of these units have come down over the past few years.

Adaptability to water temperature varies from strain to strain, but generally speaking, water you give your plants should have a temperature near 65 to 70°F.

Carbon Dioxide

CO_2 is a heavy gas. Therefore, it is better to dispense it from high up in the grow rooms for all methods. The desired CO_2 parts per million is approximately 1,500PPM: 1,100 coming from the apparatus and 400 from the outdoor air.

Carbon dioxide is most needed in the first few hours after the lights turn on.

CO_2 Production Methods

Buying a propane generator or CO_2 tank is probably the easiest way to get the desired CO_2 of 1,500PPM without using testing gear. Buying the machine preset to release the desired volume when leaving the store is important, and double-checking the figures before operating the gear is necessary, too. However, a grower should keep in mind that the generator adds heat and moisture, which may help in the winter months. Altering the climate should be considered if the range goes off somewhat. For example, humidity may rise above 60%, and therefore adding a dehumidifier or adjusting the system will lower the humidity to 40 to 70%. If a propane generator is used for the first few hours in the morning, this added heat and humidity will help open up plant stomata so that carbon dioxide intake is heightened. The propane generator can be used outside the grow room and a fan can be used to draw the carbon dioxide into the room.

A disadvantage of using CO_2 is that the exhaust fan must be shut down every time the CO_2 is being dispersed for it to be plentiful and useful to the plants. Often, the humidity rises first thing in the morning in rooms without high tech climate control. Therefore, the carbon dioxide intake can be more effective. Many growers add carbon dioxide injections for the first part of the light cycle. Some of the best grow rooms have used only the CO_2 from the great outdoors by having really strong air-intake and exhaust.

Fans are the cheapest way to bring carbon dioxide enriched air into a room and rid stagnant air from a grow room.

CO_2 can also be purchased in a two-part kit from hydroponic stores. When the powder and reactor are mixed, CO_2 is dispersed: it's cheap and easy. Supernatural Excellofizz make pucks for closets. Room temperature water is poured onto a puck to make carbon dioxide. One puck per day is used. They come in packs of 15 or 50.

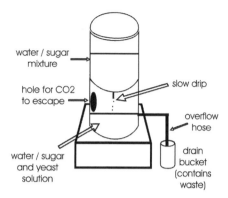

water / sugar mixture

slow drip

hole for CO2 to escape

overflow hose

water / sugar and yeast solution

drain bucket (contains waste)

It is advised to find the perfect yeast. Using a CO2 tester helps find ideal CO2 ppm

Figure 5.9: Low-tech carbon dioxide maker.

One more method of producing CO_2 is to make a water / sugar solution that drips into a lower reservoir. The lower reservoir will contain the yeast, and a water / sugar or water / molasses solution. This solution can be made to a pH of 4.0 to 5.0, which is the proper level for beer, wine, and bread yeasts. However, it will work fine if left alone.

The lower reservoir will be producing the CO_2 since it contains the yeast.

The lower reservoir should have one hole near the bottom for a siphon over-flow hose. The top of the hose will be the height of the reservoir.

A second hole should be made near the top of the lower reservoir for carbon dioxide-enriched air to escape. This hole must be higher than the siphon over-flow hole in the bottom. It can be covered with panty hose to keep out fruit flies.

One of the holes in the lid of the lower reservoir will be used to allow the solution to pour in drip-wise.

Lights and Lighting Accessories

Without light, the plants will not grow properly. With the proper amount of light at all times, plant growth can be maximized. If plants get too much light or too much heat, growth can be hindered or plants can burn out, showing a deformed flower and yellowing leaves.

Plant burnout normally happens when the most intense light from the source, like 1,000-watt sodiums, are located too close to flowers for prolonged periods. Often, only the odd flower of one plant burns out. This flower would be in the most light-intense part of the garden.

Too much light could mean other variables are not in place, such as ade-

The lower buds on larger plants—or any buds inside a plant's canopy that do not get exposed to direct lighting—will be significantly smaller than buds that receive direct light.

quate airflow or adequate CO_2 levels. However, some plants just have trouble adjusting to light intensity greater than the sun, considering it could be a new phenomena that the plant and its ancestors have never had to deal with.

When plants get too hot, the tissue hardens and changes color from green to yellow. Often, the next stage is turning from yellow to a crispy brown.

Fluorescent Lights

Fluorescent lights work well for rooting clones and starting seedlings. However, seedlings that are more than five weeks old and vigorously growing cuttings should move on to more intense light, such as a 400, 600 or 1,000-watt metal halide to get better results, and to make work in the indoor garden more simple. Plants rarely ever grow at the same rate. Therefore, constantly shuffling the height of fluorescent light fixtures and plants can be a pain in the ass. By comparison, a single halide bulb can be hung to distribute more intense light to the plants while taking up less space than fluorescent lights.

Envirolites fluorescents can be used with halides to add red light during flowering. Three 95-watt Envirolites can be used with each 1,000-watt halide. Envirolites can be used for vegetative, too. One light (1 inch above plants) can be used for every 2.6 square feet.

A grower can produce flowers from all types of fluorescent lights, but, the better grow bulbs will give more usable light, even though they are more costly. Full spectrum daylight bulbs will work and so will the combination of a cool white and a warm white bulb in a fluorescent light fixture, but the light quality will be on the marginal side. Envirolites are top-quality fluorescents.

Metal Halide Lights (Good for Vegetative Room and Flower Room)

Metal halide lights are the most versatile lights for growing flowering plants. They come in all sorts of wattages, such as 150-watt, 250-watt, 400-watt, 600-watt and 1,000-watt. The 1,000-watt bulbs are the best deal. Halides come clear coated, phosphor coated, and with specialized light spectrums. Not only are

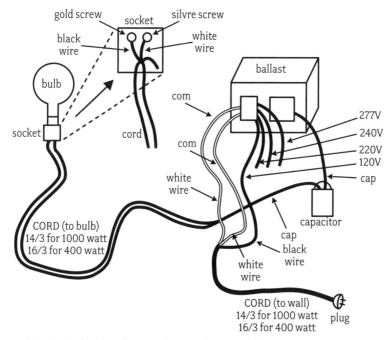

Figure 5.10: Typical wiring diagram for metal halide lights.

some bulbs more powerful per watt than others, but some also give better light. High-quality lights are available in the various watt outputs. Normally, better light costs more money. The phosphor-coated halide is one of the cheapest and most effective bulbs for vegetative growth and flowering. The color of the plants grown under the phosphor-coated bulb is pleasant on the eyes and nutrient deficiencies are easy to spot. Metal halides generally produce more blue light than red light, although some brands produce adequate levels of all parts of the light spectrum, for instance Agrosun Gold and Durotest Optimarc. In general, metal halides can be positioned closer to plants than sodium bulbs. Light intensity is one of the factors, but heat (for extended time periods) often does the most damage. A grower can get away with using only halides during vegetative growth, but at least one HPS sodium light should be added per 2 to 3 halides during flowering. Another option is adding three Envirolites per each metal halide during flowering.

High-Pressure Sodium Lights (HPS)—Flower Room Bulb

High-pressure sodium lights emit plenty of red light, but not so much blue light. They tend to be more powerful than metal halide lights, but their lack of blue light makes them best used as a partner to the metal halide light. However, used on their own, they can produce very effective results. Some sodium bulbs, such as the Son Agro Hortilux emit some bluer light. A plant can get within several inches of the hottest and most intense part of the bulb, but prolonged exposure to a near bulb will cause burning. Often a plant located a few inches from a bulb is safe for a day or two, then the bulb or plant should be moved to prevent damage. Some growers like to juggle their bulbs all over the place so they can give plants lots of intense light (from top to bottom) without burning them.

Hoods reflect light into a concentrated area. The most common hoods are parabolic hoods and horizontal hoods. Hoods, which should always be used for vegetative growth, can be used for flowering, too. Good parabolic hoods reflect usable light over more space than horizontal hoods. For vegetative growth, that is a bonus. The bulbs must be able to be placed vertically when using a parabolic hood. (Figure 5.11)

Horizontal hoods reflect concentrated light downward. These are good units in a Sea of Green system, but horizontal hoods do not cover a lot of space. However, if hoods are raised, the lights can cover more area.

Figure 5.11: Parabolic hood.

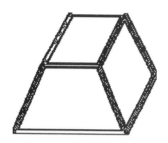

Figure 5.12: Horizontal hood.

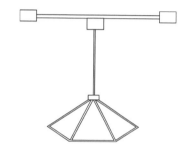

Figure 5.13: Light slides back and forth.

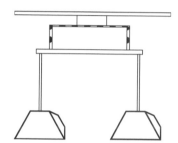

Figure 5.14: Lights are spun in a circle.

If bulbs are placed between large plants without hoods during flowering, more light can be utilized than if horizontal hoods are used. Even though the costs are a lot less, more maintenance is required.

If horizontal hoods are used, the bulbs must be the type that can be placed horizontally.

Light Movers

Light movers such as the track move lights back and forth in a straight line so as to distribute the light over a larger area, and allow bulbs to get close to plants without burning the top shoots. Circular movers move lights in a circular motion. Plants can get close to the moving bulbs and a larger area can be covered.

The downside of light movers is that control is lost regarding bulb placement. For example, placing horizontal bulbs between plants can allow for larger plants to receive more light beneath the top sections. In this case, plants can get really close to a stationary horizontal bulb, if the bulbs have cold air fanned toward them.

Light movers are good for growers with limited electricity, especially when growing small plants for large tops.

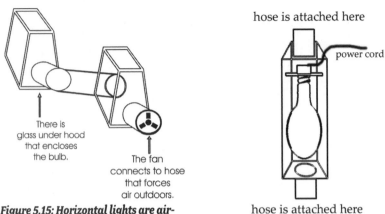

There is glass under hood that encloses the bulb.

The fan connects to hose that forces air outdoors.

hose is attached here

power cord

hose is attached here

Figure 5.15: Horizontal lights are air-cooled.

Figure 5.16: Vertical light is air-cooled.

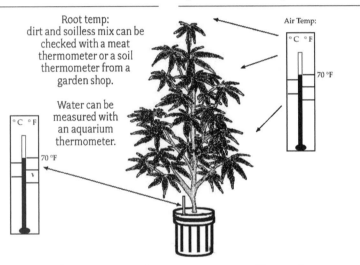

Root temp: dirt and soilless mix can be checked with a meat thermometer or a soil thermometer from a garden shop.

Water can be measured with an aquarium thermometer.

Air Temp:

°C °F

70 °F

°C °F

70 °F

Figure 5.17: Proper air temperature and root temperature contribute to vigorous growth.

Air-Cooled Lights

Air-cooled lights are halides or sodium lights that are cooled with a special hood. These hoods work well and they are affordable. There are models with no hoods, too. (Figure 5.16)

Water-Cooled Lights

Water-cooled lights use water to cool the bulbs. This type of system is rather sophisticated. These lights are an option in a hot room if cool air is not available. Water-cooled systems cost a lot of money compared to other cooling methods such as air

Commercial climate control devices.

conditioners, heat exchangers, and air-cooled lights, and many complain that water-cooled systems can pose problems for those with less technological knowledge.

Temperature

Vegetative Room Air

It is recommended that a grower keep the air temperature between 70 to 80°F at all times. The air temperature should be similar or slightly cooler during the night.

Flower Room Air

It is recommended that a grower keep the air temperature between 65 to 80°F at all times. Some strains prefer cooler nights, while others may prefer a temperature similar to the light hours.

As with growing outdoors, all-around flowering temperatures should be kept slightly cooler during flowering.

Root Temperature

Root temperature should fall between 65 and 70°F. The water temperature in a hydroponic / aeroponic system can be used to give this root temperature. A root temperature greater than 70°F can encourage fusarium.

Chillers can be used to cool hydroponic reservoirs. Heat cords can be wrapped around reservoirs or taped to the bottom of a flood table in order to increase the water / root temperature.

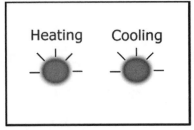

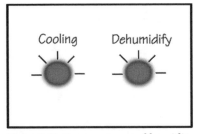

Figure 5.18: Controlling the temperature.   **Figure 5.19: Temperature and humidity control.**

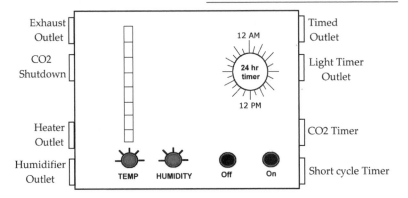

Figure 5.20: Temperature, humidity, and timer controls for various grow room items.

High-Tech Climate Control

Several companies, such as Grotek, Shiva Environmental Systems, and Green Air Products, offer various machines that run all or some of the grow equipment: exhaust fans, dehumidifiers, CO_2 units, heaters, and grow lights. With one of these units, which run a few hundred bucks, temperature, CO_2, and humidity can be maintained at relatively accurate levels at all times.

These high-tech units work well for growers with big budgets that would rather hook up equipment that will do the job, than have to fiddle with the lights and other equipment such as exhaust fans to create an ideal climate.

Calculating Power Consumption

A lot of people think the power consumption used for indoor cultivation is totally outrageous, but it really isn't. In fact, it is cheaper (while being highly productive) to run each room using the equipment described in this book than to use a small electric space heater in each room. The following is an example of calculating the energy consumed by a simple grow room as described in this chapter.

Power consumption in vegetative room (one day)

1. Exhaust fan 150-watts x 24 hours = 3.6 kW hours.
2. Two 400-watt halides 1,000-watts x 18 hours = 18.0 kW hours.
3. Oscillating fan 30-watts x 18 hours = .54 kW hours.
4. Total: 22.14 kW hours.

Potential energy competition:

Electric heater 1,500-watts x 24 hours = 36.0 kW hours.

In this case, an electric heater uses 13.86 more kW hours!

Multiplying watts by the hours of use will give the kilowatt hours. If the watts are not listed on the appliances, multiplying the volts and the amps listed on the backs of the appliances will give the wattage.

Multiplying kW hours by the electrical company's price per kW hour will give the appliance cost. For example, an oscillating fan uses 30 watts and runs for 18 hours every day. Multiplying 30 watts by 18 hours will give 540 watt hours a day, or .540 kW hours a day.

Multiplying .540 kW hours by $.05 per kW hr = $.27 a day. Then, multiplying by 30 will give the monthly cost. The monthly cost in this case is $.27 x 30 = $8.10 for a 30-day month.

Foliar Feeding Recipes

NOTE: All pH testing and the addition of pH up is optional. The results will still be beneficial if the wetting agent and / or hydrogen peroxide are left out of the recipe, but they are beneficial.

These are just a few samples. Foliar feeding should be stopped a few weeks prior to harvest so that all residues are rinsed off, and so that nutrients have time to be flushed out of the plant tissue. Flushing allows for top quality.

To protect the lungs, a respirator should be worn while foliar feeding.

Formula A

1. ½-teaspoon (3ml) of Nitrozyme or Growth Plus per quart of water.
2. 1 to 2ml of 35% hydrogen peroxide per gallon of water.
3. Organic wetting agent (manufacturer's recommended rate).

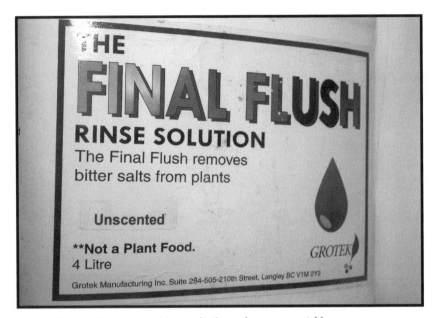

Commercial solutions remove bitter salts from plants very quickly.

---

4. 1/16-teaspoon (1/4ml) vitamin B1 per quart of water.

Optional: pH up or pH down to bring the pH to 6 to 6.5 after adding the above ingredients.

Formula B

1. Liquid kelp (recommended rate on bottle for foliar feeding.)

2. 1/2 to 1 tablespoon of Welcome Harvest Farm soluble fish powder per gallon of water.

3. 1 to 2ml of 35% hydrogen peroxide per gallon.

4. Organic wetting agent (manufacturer's recommended rate). Optional: pH up or pH down to bring the pH to 6.0 to 6.5 after adding the above ingredients

Formula C

1. Three teaspoons of liquid kelp per quart of water.

2. 1/2 to 3/4-teaspoon of Welcome Harvest Farm soluble fish powder per quart of water or 1/2 to 1-teaspoon of Alaska fish fertilizer per quart of water.

3. 1 to 2 ml of 35% hydrogen peroxide per gallon of water.

4. Organic wetting agent (manufacturer's recommended rate).

Optional: pH up or pH down to bring the pH to 6 to 6.5 after adding the above ingredients.

Hydrogen peroxide is a colorless liquid that adds valuable oxygen so that nutrient uptake is more effective and anaerobic bacteria and viruses are eliminated. Plants definitely grow faster and bigger with the use of H_2O_2, but it can be eliminated from these recipes if so desired. Warning: 35% hydrogen peroxide can burn skin and clothes on contact! Always wear strong rubber gloves and eyewear.

Hydrogen peroxide should be stored in a safe place that is not too hot. When hydrogen peroxide is kept in a hot spot, the bottle will expand. When the bottle expands, it can be tough to open without spilling the contents.

Predators

Bugs

Bugs don't seem to be a problem if the growing medium and growing conditions are at a decent standard. A little prevention can involve planting a few cloves of garlic at transplanting time, and weekly foliar feeding of liquid kelp, i.e. Nitrozyme (Growth Plus) or another brand from the time the plants are young through near maturity.

To deal with a bug problem immediately, it is recommended to apply an organic insecticidal soap combined with Nitrozyme (Growth Plus) every four to ten days while wearing a respirator. Rubbing the bottoms of the leaves gently while spraying will help to ensure that all of the areas get covered and some bugs get squished. The war psychology of bug-smearing may be argued among scientists and other interest groups.

Spider mites seem to be the rookie's most undetected predator, next to the rat. Spider mites are bugs that suck fluids from the plants, and they can spread diseases. The plants then spend time dealing with the stress, which affects yield. Understanding what makes mites thrive is half the battle. They like a hot, dry room with weak plants. They are discouraged by high humidity, and they incubate at a highly productive rate when the temperature rises above 80°F.

Spraying the undersides of the leaves well is the key, because that is where the spider mites hang. Nevertheless, if spider mites become a problem, spraying every 4 to 7 days with an organic insecticidal soap combined with ½-teaspoon per quart of Nitrozyme (Growth Plus) will help. The combination of the two is more

Sticky traps collect undesirable bugs in the grow room.

effective than straight soap. The soap should be rinsed off with plain water a couple of days after spraying to remove the soap film from the plants' stomata. Stomata are vital for transpiration. A respirator should be worn whenever fertilizers or insecticides are sprayed in order to keep the mist out of the lungs.

Another organic method for killing bugs is to use pyrethrins, which is an extract from the chrysanthemum plant. A health conscious grower probably would not want to get near the pyrethrins, organic or not. Yet another organic method to keep bugs under control are to plant garlic in soil or soilless mix. Neem oil is a good product to use to fight mites.

Other methods to kill all bugs are to use malathion, diazinon, etc. These materials have rather short half lives, but again, they stink like serious toxicity and should not have a place in the garden.

Anybody needing to use a bug spray should polish up on his horticulture skills and grow healthy plants rather than rely on a toxic Band-Aid solution.

If spider mites cannot be dealt with at this level, regular misting and foliar feeding should be enough of a preventative tactic to ensure the mite population does not get out of hand, unless plants are weak from poor cultivating methods.

Predator mites are an expensive method for dealing with the problem. If predator mites are used, it is still a good idea to lower the spider mite population with insecticides before introducing the predator mites. However, it is recommended to wait a few days for the chemical ingredients of the insecticide to wear off before the introduction of the predator mites so that they won't get zapped.

When mites are at a tolerable level, all else must be going okay. The more mite-free the rooms the better, but a grower should not be overstressed because of a few mites.

The mite population should be as minimal as possible on the mother plant(s). When a mother plant gets a disease, new clones may be hard to root. They may still be productive, but the disease will be a hindrance and can interrupt the normal schedule.

It is good to mist plants daily or every second day. A good time to mist is right after the lights come on. Misting also helps keep other bugs, such as thrips, under control.

Rats and Mice

Mice tend to like young seedlings, even those that have just germinated. However, once seedlings are 2 to 3 weeks old, mice tend to leave them alone. The seedling zone should always be well-sealed so that it is 100% mouse-proof, because they have been known to devour complete starter rooms. Utrasound is a unit that sends out a frequency that deters mice and rats, yet is not heard by pets and family.

Rats, on the other hand, can be life-threatening to plants. Rats will eat a circle around the outer stalk, at the base of the plant. This will look similar to a tree that is being cut down by a lumberjack.

This removal of the plant tissue will stop the flow of vital fluids from traveling up and down the plants, and plants will wilt and die soon afterward.

However, some plants can be saved, if they still look normal and healthy. To remedy the situation, it is recommended that you cut out a piece of outer bark from a plant of the same species; then place the patch over the bark that was eaten so that it connects to the upper and lower parts of the stalk where the rat had stopped eating.

Now just a little Vaseline and tape will secure this patchwork. This patch will act like a suspension bridge so that it is possible to pass necessary components from the lower and upper sides of the stalk. The new material will eventually be welded in place and the plant will be fine.

Mothballs around a plot may act as a deterrent to rats.

Rats do like eating some organic fertilizers such as canola meal and Flower Power.

Powdery mildew can attack some or all plants, especially in very humid grow rooms.

There are solutions for most problems in a grow room.

Mold / Mildew

It is always best to prevent mold in the bud and stems by having an acclimatized strain that is known to handle the elements, and by regular foliar feeding with Nitrozyme (Growth Plus) or a quality liquid kelp. However, for whatever reason a mold problem may occur. For mold problems, it is recommended that you spray the plants with an organic fungicide with Nitrozyme (Growth Plus). There are other fungicides that are commonly available that contain the ingredient copper sulphate, such as organic fungicides and Wilson's Bordeaux.

Grow rooms should be disinfected before they are used in order to remove any mildew / mold that creeps in during high humidity and makes a mess of the walls with black spots that leave a greasy film and stain. Keeping humidity around 60% is good prevention.

Disease

A strong strain and a good grow medium are needed at the preventative level. When a disease hits clones, starting again from seed may be the answer. Most diseases can be dealt with, unless the plant receives poor care.

Fusarium

When plants wilt not for lack of water, fusarium is a major possibility. Fusarium targets a plant with weak roots and a water temperature over 70°F. Roots often become unhealthy (brownish) in stagnant, warm water. Keeping roots healthy (whitish) and water temperature below 70°F is the best preventative measure for dealing with fusarium.

If fusarium hits a plant and it becomes wilted and sickly looking, the plant should be pulled immediately so that it will not hinder the other plants. If other plants share the same water (i.e. hydroponic gardening), hydrogen peroxide should be added to the water at a rate of 2 to 5ml / gallon to help sterilize the water.

Plants with a root disease like Fusarium and Pythium should be removed from a grow room as soon as possible; especially those that share the same recirculated nutrients.

Buds can be inspected in the plant nodes because many mold problems start there.

Pruning and Bending

Pruning is a process of pinching the top shoot(s) so that the plant will grow bushier and provide more tops, while staying shorter. Pruning is recommended if the vegetative cycle is long enough for the hormones to effectively transfer to the new set of tops (at least one month of vegetative growth after pruning is recommended). The plant hormones in the plant's top shoot are auxins, which cause a plant to grow tall. Auxins travel to the next set of top shoots after the original top shoot is removed. With pruning, auxins will form in several shoots to promote several leaders of new growth.

Pruning a month before flowering or even earlier (anywhere from two months after germination) will result in more tops. These tops may be nearly identical in size and should be close in size to that of the top had it not been pruned. Pruning may be done more than once during the vegetation process, thus creating a flower-multiplying effect. Some strains accept pruning and grow large buds, while some strains will have downsized bud production as a result of pruning. Once again, it is good to have an affiliation with and history of desired strains, so that production is maximized with pruning methods.

Bending

Bending is a process of physically moving a limb, branch, or main stalk to a new position. There are many ways of doing this. A piece of string or twine may be tied in a knot around the limb and then tied to a hook on a wall or a stake. Netting can be placed over the garden to position the limbs in a desired spot. Bending allows shoots that have been deprived of light to receive intense light. The exposed shoots can now put on mass much more quickly than when exposed to low light levels, which causes slow and unproductive growth.

Different strains grow differently in terms of the number of leaves that receive more direct light. Bending is done to obtain maximum light for the inner

Branches are tied so that the buds receive lots of light. These buds grow upward towards the light.

Broken limbs can be straightened and taped with duct tape or electrical tape if the upper growing area is not severely wilted.

vegetation and to ensure that all vegetation receives more light. Bending is a good idea indoors or out, but the limbs should not be bent too hard or beyond a point they can't take physically. Getting this right will take practice, but yields will always increase.

If a limb breaks, a grower should immediately look at the vegetation along the broken limb to see if it looks normal. If it is not wilted, then string or tape can be used to secure the break. The limb may also need careful staking. If the limb is severely wilted, cutting it off carefully will permit the plant to heal itself.

6

Harvesting, Drying, and Storing

The Plants Should be Picked When They are Ripe

How does a grower tell when his plants are ready for harvesting? Often, females have pistils that change color at maturity. Sometimes, the pistils will go from an erect white to a wrinkled brown. In some cases, the pistils will change from white to a color and finally, to brown. Either way, white or colored pistils will look rigid and alive, and brown pistils become skinny and curly. As a simple rule, the peak harvest time is when half or more of the healthy pistils become brown. However, sometimes the flowers will over-mature while still having less than half of the pistils turned brown.

When some marijuana plants over-mature, the flowers will fluff out, or become dry and old-looking. The fine line between full maturity and over-aging is often the time to pick the flowers since they are at their largest size with maximum beauty. Exact timing to pick will vary from plant to plant. Some over-mature in style and still make a wonderful flower, while some will weaken so quickly that the grade is significantly decreased.

Drying Buds

The buds can be dried in a room at 65 to 70° F and with a humidity of 30 to 50%. Buds can be dried in a hotter area to save time, but the higher heat can diminish the final quality.

Marijuana plants can be hung to dry, or picked as they dry. Hanging flowers to dry before picking is recommended for those that want to keep down the

The white hairs on the left eventually turn brown and wrinkle like those on the right.

irritating odor of handled flowers. Strains that are odor-free will still release an odor when handled, especially when they are not dry.

Flowers dry more quickly when air is moved around via an oscillating fan, even when the humidity is a little high and the temperature is cool.

Picking all buds requires removing the larger leaves in the buds, then shaving the leaf near the bud with scissors or shears.

Sweating buds after they initially dry can help pull moisture out of the stalks and into the leaf parts. Sweating can be done once, or more than once. Sweating for one day to several weeks is an option. Flowers stored with a little moisture will be better than flowers that are stored bone dry, all things being equal. However, flowers stored with too much moisture for too long can turn brown, which can lead to mold and / or rot. The line is not fine between mold and brown. However, the odor of the buds will change dra-

Left: Buds are hung to dry in a room with an odor-removing ionizer. Right: Buds are manicured as they are hung to dry.

matically when mold sets in.

Using a dehumidifier in humid areas will dramatically shorten the drying period.

Upper left: Ice water is made. Upper right: Bud and ice water mixture. Lower left: Resinous material and water is separated. Lower right: Final product.

Shake

Hash bags and pollinators can be used to get some hash from a decent supply of trim. Two books, *Hashish*, by Robert Connel Clarke and *From Trash to Stash* by Ed Rosenthal explain how to make use of lower grade leaf and trimmings. What follows below describes basic hash-making.

Basic Hash-Making Procedure

A. The weed should go into the freezer overnight, or at least for one hour.

B. The weed can be crushed up and put through a small micron window screen, such as 150 microns. The stalks and seeds that do not go through are waste products.

The green powder is the final material—press it, and you get hash balls.

C. The weed is placed in a bowl (or bucket) with chilled water that is full of ice.

D. An electric mixer is used to blend the ice and weed for 10 to 15 minutes.

E. The mixture is left to settle to the bottom for 1 to 12 hours.

F. The top mixture should be carefully removed without disturbing the bottom layer. This top mixture is waste. The next step is G, or you may choose to follow the option below.

Option
At this point the bottom mixture can be drawn through one or more smaller

Small popcorn buds can be used to make quality hash.

diameter micron bags, such as 80 or 50 microns. When a smaller micron size is used, the quality will increase, but there will be more waste. A custom bag can be made to fit snugly into the rim of a bowl, but the bottom of the bag must be higher than the bottom of the bowl so that the material falls through and settles into the bottom of the bowl. Duct tape can be used to make a quick setup.

G. The mixture should now be spooned out and placed on a coffee filter. A little water can be used to collect the remaining mixture in the bowl and this material can be run through the coffee filter.

H. The material on the filter paper is allowed to air dry.

I. Hands can be used to press the material into balls.

J. More and more force should be used to press the balls.

K. The hash balls can be stored in the freezer.

The waste leaf can be used for cooking, using 1 to 3 ounces of crushed leaf and trimmings for each pound of butter. Baker's chocolate has a good chocolate chip

Low grade buds, tiny buds, trim, and leaf can be used for making hash.

recipe that uses 1 cup of butter. Butter is simmered with crushed leaf for an hour, then strained. About 1 cup of marijuana butter is left over after the straining is completed.

Canning and Storing Dried Goods

Buds can be canned and stored in mason jars. Before storage, the jars should be washed with soap and water, then rinsed with clean water.

The next step is to boil the jars in water for 5 minutes. Then they are allowed to dry.

The dry jars should be delicately filled with the dry buds. The weight of the flowers will not change if the flowers are properly dried.

The mason jar lids should be placed in a saucepan and boiled for 3 to 5 minutes. Then, both sides of the lids should be dried with a cloth. Then the lids should be immediately placed on the jars and tightly screwed on.

The jars should be left in a cool or cold spot for a night or two.

If the lids are secured properly, the lids will be popped down, not popped up. If they are popped up, pressing each lid down with sharp, quick taps can secure the lid with a downward placement.

Finally, the jars should be stored in a cool, safe spot. The shelf life is indefinite for flowers that are properly dried.

7

Breeding

So far, this book has emphasized the use of the right strain for particular growing conditions. Now, in this chapter, we will look at some of the important factors a grower may want to know when breeding his plants.

Most plants grown these days are pure Indica, pure Sativa, or are an Indica / Sativa cross.

Although all strains have a unique set of characteristics that give a unique effect on the body, I believe that the environmental and social factors are the most important elements to say what the effects are. In fact, the same bud can pack a different buzz. The time of day, social space, friends, weather, physical demands, financial stress, tolerance, drug stacking (like coffee drinking, booze, or ephedrine consumption) are just a few of the factors which have a large influence on any buzz.

Sativa

Sativa strains tend to have small clusters of buds that extend along the branches. The buds tend to have larger spaces between the clusters than Indica strains. Often, these plants grow to a tall height.

Indica

Indica strains normally grow to be small, bushy plants with dense flowers at the tops and ends of the branches.

Indica / Sativa Crosses

These plants will look somewhere in between a pure Indica and a pure Sativa.

Breeding Decision Factors

Viable pollen (from sacks) of a male plant must contact the pistils from a female plant in order to produce seeds. The pistils of a female plant are located in the buds and at the nodes. Seeds can be made at any time the pistils are healthy, if the seeds are allowed to mature.

To determine which plants to breed, the breeder should pay attention to how successfully all the plants grow in the vegetative, early-flowering, and late-flowering states.

Good breeding insight allows for the desired traits to carry on, such as heavy-volume producing, fast maturation, low odor, potency, and a will to survive in a particular climate.

There are fancy and advanced quality traits, such as pistil colors, leaf patterns, flower density, aroma, etc. But to make this breeding discussion simple, these specific traits have been left out in favor of taking a non-rocket-science approach, based on common sense.

Plant Volume

Monitoring stalk diameters at the base of a plant and observing root mass will help in determining a larger volume plant. To accurately assess for stalk and root mass, plants should be exposed to identical growing mediums and all other variables, such as growing settings from germination throughout harvest.

In general, larger-stalked plants are harder to pull out of a container, which indicates a more elaborate root system. The root environment must be consistent in order to correctly determine root mass, because a highly oxygenated, well-fertilized root medium will allow a plant to make a more substantial root system in less space.

If small plants are preferred so that a garden needs less care, then a grower should look for small diameter stalks and less root mass. Indoor / outdoor strains with smaller stalks and less root mass will use a smaller amount of water and are not so prone to being blown over by heavy winds.

A final test in determining volume is to calculate the yield at the harvest.

For great genetics, one of the oldest and most reliable suppliers of quality plants is Sensi Seeds.

American Dream: Built for speed: two months and you could have pounds of resinous, hashy bud that gives a body / brain combo high.

Four Way: The next frontier of hybrids: four of the best Indicas blended to form a new supercannabis.

Guerrilla's Gusto: Direct from Basque battalions comes this adaptive easy-grow from Sensi. Sticky jungle buds and an intense and lengthy stone.

Hawaiian Indica: Hawaii's best Sativa blended with Sensi's finest Northern Lights results in this delectable crossover. Banana buds + massive calyxes = tropical buzz.

To get more information on these and other strains, check out www.sensiseeds.com.

Maple Leaf Indica: An Afghani-Russo-Dutch combo that results in a Canadian maple leaf pattern and a syrupy flavor.

Northern Lights: Often imitated, never duplicated. Historically used to sedate rabid elephants, the Sensi Seeds variety is almost too strong for human use.

Ruderalis Skunk: In the glory days of the Russian aristocracy, they smoked Ruderalis. Top-notch bud that can survive the harshest climes.

Super Skunk: Original Skunk backcrossed with Afghani results in this fat, stinky plant that was a Cannabis Cup winner.

Fast / Late Maturation

Choosing plants that mature quickly will allow those timing traits to be passed on to the next generation, especially if the male is a fast-maturing plant. Any inconsistencies will show up in the next generation if late- and early-maturing plants are crossed. The crossed hybrids will have varying maturing times. These days, many strains varying in potency from weak to chronic can flower in 5 to 7 weeks.

Late plants may be desired to capitalize on a strain that produces a lot of flavor.

The amount of nitrogen used during budding can alter the harvest date. Nitrogen usage during flowering will extend the flowering period, but it can increase yield if it is used to combat a nitrogen deficiency, and is not applied in excess.

Odor

Some plants will smell when they are young seedlings, some will not smell at all during their entire growth cycle. Breeding plants that don't smell allows this trait to be passed on.

Potency

THC and other chemicals are responsible for the potency of the marijuana plant. Fortunately, looking for the crystal content on the buds gives an indication of this factor. In general, when buds have lots of crystals, they are potent. Potency can also be checked with lab equipment.

Environmental Factors

Plants that belong in a particular climate will look green and strong, and have no holes in their leaves from disease or bugs. Strong plants will also adjust to and grow well in the various local weather and root conditions.

Importance of Grow Medium

Not only is the climate important in determining the ideal strain, but so is the medium below the plant. A strain grown in a soil mixture may do well in various hydroponic systems, or it may not. Some strains need more air down there than others, some more water, some more food and / or a slightly different diet. If hard work is performed on one cultivation technique, it is possible to eventually find plants that make perfect matches to various environmental conditions.

Light Levels

Plants can adapt to and utilize adverse weather to put on significant mass. Rainforest breeders have strains that grow in the cold and wet, while plants from another territory will turn pale and grow more slowly in the same adverse climate.

Continuous breeding, including inbreeding and outbreeding (unrelated crossing), can give rise to strongly acclimatized plants.

It is easier to take a plant from adverse conditions and introduce it to a warmer, less adverse climate, than to take a plant from a warm, safe environment and throw it into a rainforest jungle.

Taking plants that grow well in low-light conditions can allow an indoor grower to get a greater yield per light if the strain grows well otherwise in an indoor environment.

Also, breeding low-light plants with other plants can pass on these characteristics to the next generation. Looking at the spaces between the nodes helps in determining how well some plants use light. Less space between the nodes is preferred. When plants do not get adequate light they stretch for light. When that happens, the node spaces are increased. So, if the node space does not increase under less light, then they will grow well under the lower light level.

Disease Resistance

Root diseases such as leaf-spot fungus, exist in various soil conditions. Some strains can fight and live with the disease more easily than others.

Drought Resistance

Some plants use more water than others and their leaves, stalks, and bud mass can be inferior to a plant grown alongside in identical conditions.

Mold Resistance

Some plants can put on significant rot-free mass in cold, humid weather, while other plants will rot or form mildew under identical growing conditions.

Breeding Tips

Seedlings can run in all sorts of types. They can be hybrids with scattered genetics or purer strains with known characteristics. Good breeders generally have good seeds. Advantages of seedlings are that different strains of marijuana are possible to grow in the garden from a batch of seeds, although some seeds may be completely unproductive. If the seeds are not the predictable F1 or a pure strain, then they can give a wide assortment of varieties. Two positive aspects of a wide assortment of weed are that a grower may find a unique strain to call his own and he could have many different types of pot to smoke. Although this is not the recommended way to hit high production, the large personal bag of many different flavors and buzzes may be desired.

Easy Breeding

The easiest and safest way to produce a batch of seeds is to leave a male in another room. Then, some pollen taken from the desired male is placed on the pistils of a female plant. It is safest to pollinate a female in another location in order to produce seeds on the desired pistils of one plant, yet produce a seedless crop. Running a powerful ionizer in a grow room or near the male(s) will keep pollen out of the air.

Breeding the choice plants from seed that is continually inbred is recommended.

Making an F1 Generation

For starters, a grower should get two pure seedlots that are from different origins and grow the desired plants.

Crossing the different purebreds will make an F1 generation. This generation expresses similar-looking plants. According to Mendel, this generation is all the same because the dominant genetic makeup is expressed. Many seed companies sell F1 seeds; some use genetic mapping to make sure that all the seeds are the same. For example, one parent of the F1 generation could be a pure strain like White Widow and the other variety could be a pure strain like Skunk #1.

This generation can exhibit hybrid vigor, which means that they have more genetic potential to grow bigger and stronger than the pure strains.

Making a Purebred
Inbreeding / Outbreeding a Pure Strain

Another way to make a pure strain is to inbreed or outbreed the seeds from a pure strain. This can be thought of in terms of dogs; two German Shepherd dogs will make German Shepherd puppies.

Inbreeding a Hybrid

In many cases a grower has seeds that come from an unknown origin or sloppy breeding. A grower can inbreed these seeds for several (i.e. 4 to 6) generations until they all show the same traits under identical growing conditions.

Experimental Hermaphrodite Results

Plants that have been crossed using a chosen hermaphrodite and a strong genetically different female (without hermaphroditic characteristics) can be best, although the most difficult to make.

Hermaphrodites (also called hermes) can look almost entirely female, with only a few male pollen sacks. On the other hand, hermaphrodites can look nearly completely male, with only a few small buds that easily go unnoticed. Or hermaphrodites can look somewhere in between male and female by having a decent supply of male pollen and female flowers.

The cross between a female cutting and its mother that was shocked into hermaphroditism creates stability in the seed line, yet can produce a risky supply of hermaphrodite offspring. Seeds made from hermaphroditic pollen can produce more females than crosses from a single male and single female source, in most cases. Generally, self-pollinated hermaphrodites make less female seed and more hermaphrodites than a cross between a hermaphrodite and a non-hermaphroditic female. Hermaphrodites are a touchy issue.

Hermaphroditic breeding results can be different from strain to strain. Female plants that were offspring from hermaphrodite pollen have the potential to turn hermaphroditic when they over-mature.

Many growers like to stay a mile away from hermaphroditic crosses because they can be a risk to the seed grower who wants flowers without seeds. Since hermaphroditism is often triggered by events such as environmental conditions, hermaprodites can be time bombs when used anywhere but in a controlled environment. Often, though, hermes will only produce the odd pollen sack that will make a seed or so at the plant nodes. Some growers that make female seed will often pick a male and female from that seed lot and inbreed them in order to reduce potential hermaphrodite problems, yet have a supply of consistent seeds.

The question many would ask is, Why play around with hermaphrodites to achieve a higher female count, when sexing plants and cloning is so easy?

Making Hermaphrodites from Females

Here is one method for forcing indoor / outdoor plants to turn hermaphroditic. At outdoor harvest time, a grower can harvest the plant, while making sure to leave some lower vegetation so it can be rejuvenated back into a vegetative state indoors. If this outdoor plant is transplanted from a permanent site to a container, then placed indoors to rejuvenate back with an 18-hour photoperiod, and flowered again at 12 hours when there is plenty of new growth, it may produce seed. It takes about three weeks to a month to begin the rejuvenation process. Before the rejuvenation takes place, the plant will look like it has no growth potential. One experiment of this type resulted in four hermaphrodites from four transplants.

It is important to always watch for hermaphroditic qualities in all aspects of growing, because hermes can easily go undetected and produce unwanted seed. Some hermaphrodites show female traits throughout early flowering, then suddenly produce an unexpected male flower on the top. With correct timing, it is possible to pull off the unopened pollen sacks so that other females near the plant won't produce seed.

Seed Storage

Mature seeds can be saved, the immature seeds can be discarded. Immature seeds will look white and / or pale green. Mature seeds are brown with black specks. The time when the buds are picked often affects the quality of seed.

Seeds can be stored in an airtight glass container like a canning jar or a ginseng vial with a rubber stopper. Little vials are nice for the ease of keeping tabs on several varieties. Containers should always be labeled immediately in order to keep accurate records.

Once the seeds are in glass, they can be put in the freezer, wrapped in plastic and buried in the ground, or stored in some other cool, dry, dark place.

Seeds should be stored at least one month before germinating. They can last several years in storage and still have high germination rates. On the other hand, beautiful-looking seeds that have been stored properly can have low germination rates. Germination rates lower as the seeds age, although some strains have longer shelf lives than other ones. In fact, some strains have the ability to have high germinating rates after years of storage at room temperature.

Before seeds are relied on for an entire crop, it helps to know how well they germinate. As time rolls on, the seeds can be germinated from time to time to see how well they germinate.

8

Composting

Composting allows a grower to fertilize his buds with food waste. If the food is not composted it is sent to the landfill and helps out nobody. But, if it is composted indoors or outside, the result is a ready-made plant food. Compost is very easy to use. A grower can add compost to quality dirt and get quality bud.

There are two standard methods types of composting: heated compost and worm composting.

Heated Compost

Making hot compost involves using aerobic bacteria to break down food scraps, etc., and turning it into usable compost. Hot compost can be made in as little as 2 to 8 weeks. The temperature of the compost pile is the key. The temperature of the compost pile can be between 100 and 160°F. A rod can be purchased to determine the temperature, or feeling by hand is an option. Turning the compost regularly and adding materials such as perlite, sawdust, and peat moss helps to add aeration for the bacteria to the pile. Adding an organic peroxide such as calcium peroxide adds oxygen and lime to the pile. When the bacteria thrive, compost breakdown will happen faster.

Hot composting is a good method for an impatient gardener that wants usable compost as soon as possible.

Worm Composting

Worm composting consists of using worms to consume food scraps, digest dirt and other materials, and then excrete worm castings, which is a rich fertilizer that contains most plant loving elements like nitrogen, trace elements, and humic acids. The key to using worms is to provide them with the proper temperature in the compost (60 to 75°F). The worms will reproduce and be most productive in this range.

When the worms have done their job of making the compost , they should be taken out of the bin and placed in a pile. Then, a light or sunlight should be allowed to shine on the pile. The light will make the worms repel downward into the pile. Now, the compost which contains organic matter and worm castings can be collected from the top portion of the pile. This is a great way to make organic matter and worm castings, which cost an arm and a leg at the local garden centers, cheaply.

Making a Compost Bin

Bin construction is standard for hot composting or worm composting. A compost bin can be made using five pieces of wood or steel that are 3 feet square. A matching lid may be added if a bin is used. Nice, rich-looking, fine black dirt can be layered on the bottom 2 to 8 inches. A well-draining piece of ground (no bin) works, too.

Add vegetable, fruit, and seafood scraps that break down relatively easily. Scraps can be blended or put through a food processor to speed up the process.

As soon as the layer of food scraps is 2 to 8 inches high, it should be covered with a 1 to 4-inch dirt layer. If worm composting is the plan, a grower should place a few hundred to a thousand worms (i.e. Red Wigglers or African Night Crawlers) into the bin. People raise worms, and fisherman supply guys sell them. Adding common earthworms from the yard will work, too, but they are slower to reproduce and will be less thorough eaters. If the soil is already nice and wormy in that location, many more worms will be attracted to the compost pile. This cycle can now go on and on (dirt, food scraps, dirt, food scraps). The worms are added only once.

The worm population will multiply in time, and taking worms from one compost pile and adding them to a new one is an option, so that piles can decompose on a predictable schedule to allow for usable compost in the garden.

It is recommended that you turn the contents of each compost bin with a pitchfork or claw periodically to help speed up the breakdown process and add air to the composted blend. For hot composting, a pile can be turned every day, every few days, or every week. A compost bin or pile can break down completely in two weeks to a few months, depending on the pile temperature and quality of compost pile. The composted material can be made more fertile by adding dolomite lime (one or more cups), manure (up to a full bag) when the fine dirt is added, and / or the odd dose of cottonseed meal.

Tips: During the cold of winter, a decent layer of straw on top of the pile is needed so the worms will have warmth and will stay in the higher spots of the compost pile to break down new food scraps. The pile should stay moist. It should not be allowed to dry out, but it shouldn't be allowed to become waterlogged either.

Indoor Worm Bin

The four main items a vermicompost maker needs are a box, bedding, red wiggler worms, water, and food waste. Any wood or plastic box that is 2x2 feet and 7 to 9 inches high will work fine. If a plastic tub like a Rubbermaid is used, small holes should be made in the bottom for drainage using a small drill bit or sharp knife. Something should be placed underneath the box to collect the runoff moisture so that it won't stain the floor. An easy bedding mix is probably kicking around the house, such as 70% shredded paper product like corrugated cardboard, newspaper, or letter paper, to be combined with 30% peat moss. Since composting is being done with the red wiggler manure worm, the bedding could have any percentage of manure. Some worm raisers feed their worms composted livestock manure to eat up their smelly livestock crap and get back nice, black gold worm castings. If straight manure is used, it should be composted, not fresh and hot. The worm castings may be excrement from the worms, but they do not stink.

A half cup of dirt can be added to the box, too, so that grit is available for the worms' gizzards.

The whole blend should be mixed thoroughly and moistened with a few gallons of water. Then, the worms can be added. The beds should never dry out or become over-saturated because that is not the desired habitat of the red wiggler. The box should be covered because the worms do not like light.

With a 2x2-foot bin, you should imagine dividing it into 9 equal parts, which would look like an Xs and Os game. Every time a small bucket of compost is full in the kitchen, it can be buried into one of the nine equal parts. After filling all nine sites, the process can be repeated so that all of the bedding and garbage is converted into compost.

At this point, all of the product can be used for the plants. Or, half of the compost can be moved into another compost bin while the other half of the bin is filled with new bedding. Now, there are two boxes with compost and fresh bedding. After this new bedding has made new compost, half of the castings can be used for the garden and the process can be repeated. Or, this effect can be multiplied and you can have four boxes on the go. When you have enough boxes and sufficient garbage, you can make a continual supply of compost by using half for the garden and the other half as starting material.

Red wigglers require a temperature between 60 to 75°F to be productive eaters and rapidly reproductive. If the area is cold, a thermostatically controlled heat cord can be wrapped around the box to keep the worm bin warm. Some horticulture heat cords are thermostatically controlled at 72°F. Another option is to place a heat pad under a bin that is placed on 2x4s. Heat pads are available at drug stores.

This is small scale compost making, but it could make enough fertilizing material to grow enough bud for personal use.

Compost Turners

A ComposTumbler can be purchased to make compost quickly, and with no mess. These are bins that heat the compost materials up to speed up the break-down process. They are less than $200, and can be of extreme value in an apartment. A grower could make all his fertilizer with this unit, if a fresh food diet was part of his equation.

You can also build your own compost turner.

Building a Compost Turner

A real cheap method for making an easy to turn bin is to use a garbage can as the source for holding the compost.

Materials

1. Strong plastic garbage can (15 to 40-gallon).
2. Twelve 2-foot pieces of 1½-inch PVC.
3. Eight 1-foot pieces of 1½-inch PVC.
4. Eight 1½-inch PVC elbows.
5. Four 1½-inch PVC Ts.
6. Six eye-hooks.
7. Three bungy cords.

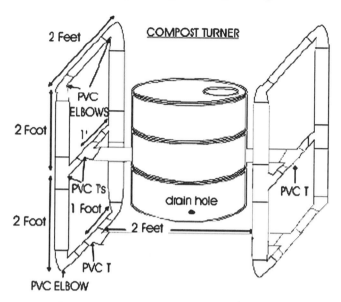

Figure 8.1: A garbage supported by a PVC frame becomes a compost turner.

Procedure

A. A hole should be drilled with a 2 to 3-inch holesaw, halfway from the bottom of the can. Now the can should be rotated 180° and another hole drilled at the same height.

B. One of the 2-foot PVC pieces runs through the middle. This will support the can.

C. Another 2-foot piece of PVC runs under the can parallel to the 2-foot piece that runs through the can.

D. All four ends of the 2-foot PVC pieces are connected to the PVC Ts.

E. The 1-foot lengths are connected to the T-ends.

F. Now the elbows are connected the exposed ends of the 1-foot lengths.

G. Connect the rest of the 2-foot pieces to the rest of the PVC elbows.

H. Now the elbows should be placed to connect the vertical 2-foot PVC pieces to the horizontal 1-foot pieces.

I. The eye-hooks should be inserted evenly around the diameter of the bucket. Bungy cords will be used to secure the lid when the container is flipped over and over to allow for aeration.

J. The last step is to drill a 1-inch hole at the bottom of the can to allow for drainage.

This bin can now be used for hot composting or worm composting. For hot composting, it should be rotated frequently, such as every day, every few days, or once a week.

9

Troubleshooting

General Indoor Cultivation Problems, Causes, and Remedies

Problem: Plants turn yellow at any time during all growth phases, less during the final two weeks of the flowering period.

Cause: Lack of light, lack of nutrition, or a poor climate.

Remedy:

A. The lights should be put at the recommended distances as mentioned in the guide on pages 13 and 27. Light levels must be extremely poor for this to occur, because most plants will stay green and use less nutrient if grown in shady areas.

The only time the leaves should lighten and become yellow is during late flower.

Yellowing is possible under inadequate fluorescent lighting for specific strains. Hopefully, the pH of soil or nutrient solution is adequate.

B. For nutrition problems the plants should be fed with a balanced nutrient formulation as discussed in chapters 1 and 5; the medium should be well flushed, and a proper nutrient formulation should be added a few days later.

This is the best way to deal with nutritional problems because it is very difficult to determine one deficiency from another. Also, salts clogging up the soil may be inhibiting the plant from getting what it needs because nutrients are locked up.

C. For the climate, good air should enter into the room and bad air should go out. Temperature and humidity should fall within the limits described on pages 5, 9, and 215. Again, if the plants get fed right, the pH is good, the grow medium is not over-toxified, and the climate is proper, then normal feeding will be in the plants' best interest. If a plant is not recovering after this treatment, it has probably been weakened and / or stressed to the point of no return.

After plants have been treated with a proper diet, the top leaves and new leaves should be watched for the color. The old leaves may not green up. Old leaves will reach a point of yellowness and cannot turn around. This is a fine line.

Nitrogen is the most common deficiency that hits the older leaves (further toward the bottom of the plant). If the leaves are yellowing just slightly and plants are well-fed, then they should revive to a green color in less than a week.

The first sign of over-fertilization is burnt leaf tips, followed by speckled and discolored leaves that will become crispy and die.

Problem: Plant tips burn.

Cause: Light is too close to plant tops, or plants may have been over-fertilized with a product such as humic acid.

Remedy: Lights should be positioned at the recommended levels. For over-fertilization, flush each plant with several gallons (in soil / soilless) or a full reservoir of plain water (hydroponics) immediately.

Over-watering a plant can cause damping off, which rots the stalk and makes the plant collapse.

Problem: Clones dry up and look near death.

Cause: Lid was not placed properly on the flat or it has holes in it, plants may not have been misted at regular intervals, or the heat pad thermostat may be malfunctioning. Rooting medium has dried up.

Remedy: Clones should be misted regularly and close attention should be paid so that the rooting medium stays moist. New clones may have to be cut if they are beyond the point of becoming healthy.

Problem: Germinated seedlings didn't sprout through the mix, although everything was done as instructed in chapter 1.

Cause: Mouse / mice dug into mix and ate fresh shoots.

Remedy: It is recommended that you start over with a mouse-proofed grow area, created by making a barrier to entry such as a wood or plastic wall.

Problem: Seedlings grew tall and spindly and are flopping over.

Cause: Light levels are not sufficient: i.e. fluorescents or halides are too high above the plants.

Remedy: The seedlings should be transplanted into larger pots and the stalks should be buried up to their first set of leaves. A grower should make sure that the light distances are as recommended: 1 to 2 inches for flouros, 1½ to 2 feet for 400-watt halides.

Problem: Fertilizer bags were broken into.

Cause: Rats like several types of organic fertilizers, such as canola meal and Flower Power.

Remedy: Fertilizers should be stored in a totally enclosed area.

Problem: Some plant leaves have many holes, with or without bugs present.

Cause: Bugs or a disease. Certain strains develop bug and disease problems more than others.

Remedy:

A. For bugs, Nitrozyme (Growth Plus) with organic insecticidal soap may be used as spelled out on pages 219-220.

B. Leaf spot fungus may show up whether or not the mix is contaminated. The inner parts of the leaves begin to rust, then the material falls out and leaves holes. To deal with the problem, 2 to 5ml / gallon of 35% hydrogen peroxide can be used during watering, and calcium peroxide can be added to soilless mix / soil before it is reused. Leaf spot fungus problems are unpredictable. It will attack weak or healthy-looking plants. For example, in a six-plant garden, one or more plants may have the disease, while the others will show no signs at all.

Problem: Indoor plant leaves have silver spots.

Cause: Spider mites have moved in.

Remedy: It is recommended that you spray with Nitrozyme (Growth Plus) and organic insecticidal soap every 4 to 7 days and spray with plain water daily during the vegetative phase. Spraying with Nitrozyme (Growth Plus) and organic insecticidal soap every six days and with plain water two days later for budding plants before the final two weeks of flower is a safe choice. There are other insecticides that work, such as Malathion, Diazinon, pyrethrins, etc., but they are more toxic to handle. Respirators should be worn when using toxic sprays. Toxic sprays should not be applied too close to harvest as they can leave residues. It is best to use only plain water no more than twice a week during the last two weeks before harvest to prevent mold.

Also, it is recommended that you check regularly to see that humidity is not below 40% and temperature not above 80°F. Also, adding or decreasing gadgets like humidifiers, dehumidifiers, air-conditioners, or heaters may be needed to achieve the optimal levels, as described on pages 5,9 and 215.

Problem: Breaker keeps blowing.
Cause: Too much gear is being used at one circuit.
Remedy: Other outlets that are on a different breaker should be used; wiring may need to be extended or an extension cord may need to be used. Using less gear can help solve this problem.

Hot temperatures, over-mature buds, and small buds that do not receive direct light can become crispy, impotent, and dry.

Problem: Plants look abnormal in growth from others that are treated the same.
Cause: Seedling cannot thrive under such conditions.
Remedy: Using the right strain is more than half the battle.

Problem: Plant fell over.

Cause: Too much mass, or the plant is weak and living under inadequate conditions, whether it be a poor diet, a poor climate, disease, or bugs.

Remedy:

A. Grower should learn to prune and bend to support the plants.

B. For a proper diet, the plants should be nurtured with correct feeding and proper pH so that the harvest is a healthy one. There are feeding samples in chapter 5.

C. The plants should be given a proper environment as explained in detail in chapter 5.

Problem : Plants grew tall but produced very few flowers.

Cause: Weak lighting and / or improper feeding during flowering.

Remedy: Plants should be allowed to get adequate light and nutrition. Chapters 1, 2, and 5 explain correct lighting; chapter 5 explains feeding.

Glossary

Acidic A solution or soil is acidic when the pH is less than 7.0.

Aeroponics A growing system in which plant roots are fed with a misted solution. An aeroponic system is similar to a misting system that is used in a supermarket to spray vegetables.

Alkaline A solution or soil is alkaline when the pH is greater than 7.0.

Bale A large bag of compressed soilless mix.

Breeding Making seeds from male pollen and female pistils.

Budding The process of producing flowers.

Bypass valve A valve above a pump which allows the solution to flow through another tube so that the flow can be controlled in the main header line.

Calibrating Setting a tds pen or ph meter so that its readout is the same as the "known" testing solution.

Carbon Dioxide A gas with one carbon ion and two oxygen ions.

Circular mover A light mover which spins in a circle, much like a ceiling fan.

Clone A new plant that has the same genetic make up as the mother plant.

Cloning Making an identical genetic copy of the mother plant.

Column system A gardening system for which plants are stacked directly above each other.

Composting Recycling household waste in order to make fertilizer. Cutting see clone

Dehumidifier A machine which reduces the humidity in the air.

Desalinizing Removing salt from water.

Element A specifuc atom or ion found in the periodic table of elements.

Exhaust fan A fan which removes air from a room and sends it elsewhere.

Feeder line The small tubing that delivers solution to a plant.

F1 The offspring of a cross from two pure strains.

Feeding Giving plants their desired plant food.

Flowering The process of producing flowers.

Flood table A hortcultural waterproof table with four sides that can hold and drain nutrients when desired.

Flooding and Draining Feeding plant roots with a solution that floods a table, then drains back into a reservoir.

Flower forcing Altering light photoperiods to induce a plant to flower.

Flushing Removing salts from a growing medium. Flushing is also a process of removing elements from the leaves and flowers too.

Foliar feeding Applying liquid plant fertilizer to leaves.

Fungicide A gardening material that is used to get rid of and control mold and mildew problems.

Germinating Bringing a seed to life.

Header line The larger tubing that is connected to the pump and smaller, individual feeder lines.

Hermaphrodites Plants that have both male and female reproductive parts.

High tech climate control A computerized machine which controls various pieces of equipment to reach specific grow room conditions; like temperature and humidity.

Holesaw A round saw which can be attached to a drill to make round holes in wood, plastic, and metal.

Hood A covering for a bulb which reflects light.

Humidity It is a measurement of the percentage of moisture that is in the- air.

Hydroponics Feeding plants with a nutrient solution in a medium that does not contain soil.

Inline filter A filter which fits inside tubing to trap particles.

Insecticide A product that is used to deal with a bug problem in the garden.

Kilowatt One thousand watts.

Kilowatt hour One thousand watts of electricity usage in one hour of time.

Line Punch A tool used to make holes for small barbed or threaded fittings.

Medium The material a plant is grown in, such as soilless mix, perlite, rockwool, and coconut fibers.

Misters Miniature spray guns which are inserted into the ends of tubing that convert pressurized solution into a fine mist.

Mother plant A plant which is used to cut identical cuttings.

Neutral ph A solution, soil, or medium with a ph of 7.0

NFT Feeding plants with a liquid nutrient that runs down the bottom of a trough.

Organic Naturally occuring fertilizers.

Organic hydroponics A process of growing in naturally occuring materials that do not contain dirt.

Overflow hose A piece of tubing used as a precaution on a hydroponic flood table. The tubing allows solution to drain back into the reservoir if it gets too high on the flood table.

Parts per million (PPM) This is the amount of 1 part of something in a million parts of another. In terms of fertilizer, 1,500PPM means there are 1,500 parts of fertilizer in 1,000,000 parts of water.

Perpetual harvesting A growing system in which buds are harvested continually, rather than all at the same time.

Pesticides Materials which are used to stop gardening problems; such as a fungicide or insecticide.

pH The acidity of a solution. 7.0 is neutral, <7.0 is acidic and >7.0 is alkaline.

PH buffered In horticulture, a ph buffered solution has an ingredient which allows a solution to keep a constant ph.

PH down A horticultural ingredient that is used to lower the ph in a solution.

PH drift A ph which moves up or down.

PH up A horticultural ingredient that is used to raise the ph in a solution.

Picking Removing undesirable fan leaves and other leaves to get "aesthetically pleasing" buds.

Pistil The hairs protruding from female plants (mainly buds) which can be pollinated to make seeds.

Plywood Common layered wood used for construction.

Pollen The fertilizing element of a flowering plant.

Predator Another living organism that targets the plant in order to feed and often weakens or kills it in the process.

Pruning Removing top and side shoots in order to produce a bushier plant.

Pure Strain Plants that breed identical-like offspring.

PVC Commercial plastic tubing often used in plumming applications.

Reflectix A commercial insulation material that reflects light.

Rejuvenating Bringing a harvested plant back into vegetative growth.

Reservoir The tank that holds nutrient solution in a hydroponic/aeroponic system.

Rockwool A common commercial fiberglass-like hydroponc medium which holds lots of water and air.

Rooting The process of a clone forming new roots.

Seedlings Young plants that were started from seed. The seedling phase lasts somewhere near 5 weeks before the plants grow at a fast rate.

Sexing Forcing a seedling to show it reproductive organs.

Shoots The new plant growth that extends from branches.

Soilless mix A growing medium that is mainly composed of peat moss, perlite, and lime.

Stove pipe Commercial wood stove piping that comes in sizes like 5-inch and 6-inch in diameter, and 4-ft to 5-ft in length.

Strain A variety of cannabis, such as Timewarp and Blueberry.

Sweating Drawing moisture from the stalks of dried flowers.

Thru-hull fitting A pvc fitting with threads and a nut. It is like a hollow nut and bolt.

Top-feeding Applying a nutrient solution from the top of the growing medium.

Track A light mover which moves slowly back and forth over a set distance.

Training Positioning limbs with string, netting and plant yo-yos in order to allow the plant to receive more light.

Transplanting Moving plants into a new medium.

Vegetative growth The growth phase before plants produce buds.

Vertical garden A horticulture garden where plants are stacked on top of each other.

Wick system A simple, pumpless hydroponic system which uses a wick and capillary action to feed and water plants.

Worm castings Manure from earthworms.

Index

Also available from Green Candy Press

Marijuana Cooking:
Good Medicine Made Easy
by Bliss Cameron and
Veronica Greene

Bliss Cameron and Veronica Green guide would-be chefs through the process of making their own tasty and healthy home remedies using marijuana as the main ingredient. Step-by-step, high quality photographs grace nearly every page, walking readers through the creation of such recipes as recipes Bliss Balls, Butterscotch Blondies, and Honey Chocolate Brownies. $14.95

The Good Bud Guide
by Albie

Designed like a guide to fine wines, this handy book itemizes and profiles a wide range of marijuana strains, each one accompanied by an educated evaluation of its aroma, taste, and effect. High-quality glossy images and precise growing information help discerning enthusiasts identify the best-bred bud and perhaps even grow their own. The most comprehensive strain guide every produced. $19.95

Cannabis Breeder's Bible
by Greg Green

This groundbreaking guide to breeding covers all the inside dope: new hybridization techniques, international seed law issues, protecting new breeds or strains from knockoff artists, shipping seeds and clones, breeding lab designs, product testing, primordial cannabis, landrace and lost strains, common mutations, and more. $21.95

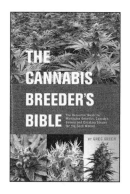

Order by phone at 916-577-1226

Also available from Green Candy Press

Greetings From Cannabis Country

Shot at Trichome Technologies, home to the world's largest growing system and highest grades of marijuana, these photo-postcards showcase 14 different strains of the plant. A must for enthusiasts, Greetings from Cannabis Country includes full-color shots of lush specimens set dramatically against dark backgrounds, intense close-ups with fascinating detail, and panoramas of crops ready to harvest. $11.95

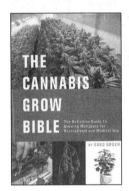

The Cannabis Grow Bible
by Greg Green

This guide offers methods for growers who want to maximize the yield and potency of their crop. It explains the "Screen of Green" technique that gives a higher yield using fewer plants, an important development for American growers who, if caught, are penalized according to number of plants. The Cannabis Grow Bible is an authoritative source that features almost 200 color and black-and-white photographs, charts, and tables. With an emphasis on the day-to-day aspects of maintaining a garden and European expertise, this book ensures that growers will enjoy a successful harvest. $21.95

The Marijuana Chef Cookbook
by S.T. Oner

High rollers looking for something more adventurous than The Joy of Cooking will find it in The Marijuana Chef Cookbook. This guide to cannabis cuisine takes satisfying the munchies to a new level. In addition to such scrumptious and imaginative recipes as Primo Poultry, Nutter Butter, Midnight Pizza, Primeval Pasta, and Chocca Mocha, the book covers potency issues, health information, legal tips, and a culinary history of the weed. $13.00

Available from www.greencandypress.com

Also available from Green Candy Press

Cannabis Cultivation
by Mel Thomas

Written by commercial-scale grower Mel Thomas — nicknamed "Mr. Big" by the authorities — Cannabis Cultivation divulges the expertise, tips, and insight he learned at the helm of one of the world's largest marijuana growing operations. Free of technical jargon and boring theory, the book's step-by-step directions enable anyone to grow and harvest the highest quality marijuana using simple techniques and inexpensive, everyday gardening tools. All of the important factors that influence growth rate, yield, and potency are covered, including lighting, planting mediums, pH, nutrients, water systems, air, and temperature. $16.95

Marijuana Outdoor Grower's Guide
by S.T. Oner

More than just a grow book, Marijuana Outdoor Grower's Guide provides easy-to-follow instructions and sensible advice on growing marijuana the natural way. Special emphasis is placed on organic and natural methods so that medicinal users need not worry about harmful chemicals. With a focus on simple growing techniques and the hands-on aspects of maintaining a garden, even newbies can enjoy a successful harvest. $13.00

Order by phone at 916-577-1226